LABORATORY Manual

# SCIENCE

CBSE Class IX

# LABORATORY Manual

# SCIENCE

## CBSE Class IX

*Authors*
Priyasha Gupta (Physics)
Abhishek Gupta (Chemistry)
Richa Raj (Biology)

Name........................................................................................

Class........................ Section........................Roll No........................

School......................................................................................

arihant
SUCCESS AND NOTHING LESS

Arihant Prakashan (School Division Series)

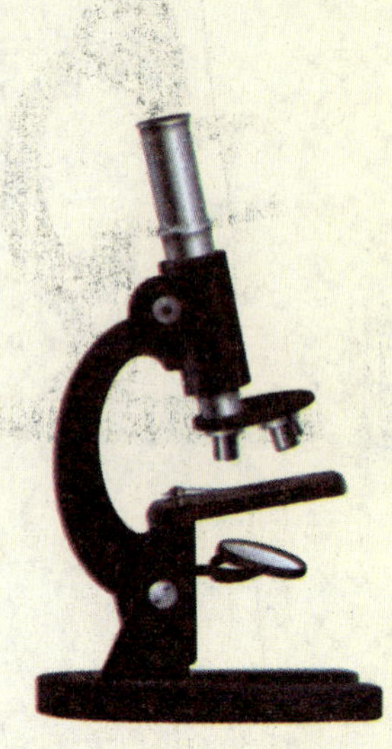

**Arihant Prakashan** (School Division Series)

## ✡ Administrative & Production Offices

**Regd. Office**
'Ramchhaya' 4577/15, Agarwal Road, Darya Ganj, New Delhi -110002
Tele: 011- 47630600, 43518550; Fax: 011- 23280316

**Head Office**
Kalindi, TP Nagar, Meerut (UP) - 250002, Tel: 0121-7156203, 7156204

## ✡ Sales & Support Offices

Agra, Ahmedabad, Bengaluru, Bareilly, Chennai, Delhi, Guwahati, Hyderabad, Jaipur, Jhansi, Kolkata, Lucknow, Nagpur & Pune

✡ **Price :** ₹ 375.00

**PO No. :** TXT-29-T071423-6-26

Published by Arihant Publications (India) Ltd.

For further information about the books from Arihant, log on to **www.arihantbooks.com** or email to **info@arihantbooks.com**

Follow us on    

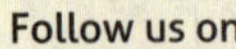

# Contents



## LIST OF EXPERIMENTS

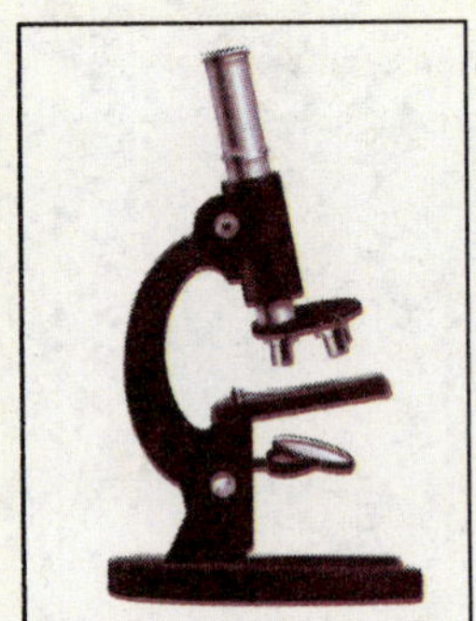

N
S

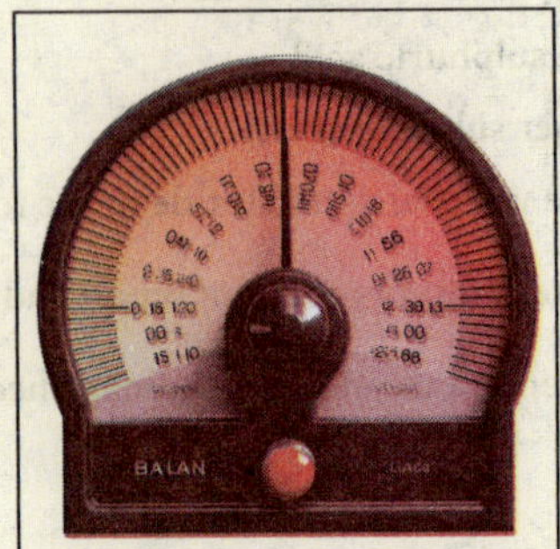

BALAN

# Syllabus

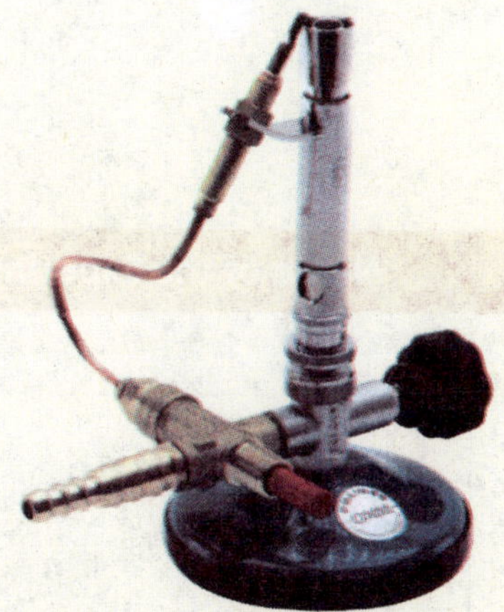

## PRACTICAL

1. Preparation of **Unit I**
   a) a true solution of common salt, sugar and alum.
   b) a suspension of soil, chalk powder and fine sand in water.
   c) a colloidal solution of starch in water and egg albumin/milk in water and distinguish between these on the basis of
      - transparency
      - filtration criterion
      - stability

2. Preparation of **Unit I**
   (a) a mixture
   (b) a compound
   using iron filings and sulphur powder and distinguishing between these on the basis of:
   (i) appearance, i.e. homogeneity and heterogeneity
   (ii) behaviour towards a magnet
   (iii) behaviour towards carbon disulphide as a solvent
   (iv) effect of heat

3. Perform the following reactions and classify them as physical or chemical changes : **Unit I**
   (a) Iron with copper sulphate solution in water
   (b) Burning of magnesium ribbon in air
   (c) Zinc with dilute sulphuric acid
   (d) Heating of copper sulphate crystals
   (e) Sodium sulphate with barium chloride in the form of their solutions in water.

4. Preparation of stained temporary mounts of (a) onion peel, (b) human cheek cells & to record observations and draw their labelled diagrams. **Unit II**

5. Identification of Parenchyma, Collenchyma and Sclerenchyma tissues in plants, striped, smooth and cardiac muscle fibers and nerve cells in animals from prepared slides. Drawing of their labelled diagrams. **Unit II**

6. Determination of the melting point of ice and the boiling point of water. **Unit I**

7. Verification of the laws of reflection of sound. **Unit III**

8. Determination of the density of solid (denser than water) by using a spring balance and a measuring cylinder. **Unit III**

9. Establishing the relation between the loss in weight of a solid when fully immersed in **Unit III**
   (a) tap water
   (b) strongly salty water, with the weight of water displaced by it by taking at least two different solids.

10. Determination of the speed of a pulse propagated through a stretched string / slinky (helical spring). **Unit III**

11. Verification of the law of conservation of mass in a chemical reaction. **Unit III**

# INDEX

| S.No. | Name of the Experiment | Page No. | Date | Remarks |
|---|---|---|---|---|
| | | | | |

# INDEX

| S.No. | Name of the Experiment | Page No. | Date | Remarks |
|---|---|---|---|---|
| | | | | |

# INDEX

| S.No. | Name of the Experiment | Page No. | Date | Remarks |
|---|---|---|---|---|
| | | | | |
| | | | | |
| | | | | |
| | | | | |
| | | | | |
| | | | | |
| | | | | |
| | | | | |
| | | | | |
| | | | | |
| | | | | |
| | | | | |
| | | | | |
| | | | | |
| | | | | |
| | | | | |
| | | | | |
| | | | | |
| | | | | |
| | | | | |
| | | | | |
| | | | | |
| | | | | |
| | | | | |
| | | | | |
| | | | | |
| | | | | |
| | | | | |
| | | | | |

LABORATORY Manual

# SCIENCE

# CERTIFICATE

This is to certify that Experiments recorded in this Practical Notebook have been performed by ______________________ (Student's name)

of __________ (class/section) of ______________________ (school name)

during academic session ______________

.................................... Examiner Signature

.................................... Principal Signature (with school stamp)

.................................... Teacher Signature

# General Introduction of Laboratory Work

## Introduction

Experiments play an important role in the progress of science, as a large number of inventions and path breaking discoveries have been possible through investigations that are usually carried out in laboratories. A school science laboratory is a place, where basic experimental skills are learnt by performing a set of prescribed experiments.

Seeing experiments being performed (demonstration experiments) is quite important for the understanding of the principles of science, but performing experiments by one's own hands is not only a thrilling experience but is also important because it entails "learning by doing". It also helps in understanding the concepts of science.

The experiments prescribed in the syllabus intend to develop basic skills of measurement, handling of some common measuring instruments, equipment and chemicals, setting simple apparatus, handling microscope and preparing slides, making observations, collecting data and presenting it in appropriate format, interpreting and drawing their conclusions and result.

## General Laboratory Facilities

A science laboratory is fully equipped with working tables, items of common utility and space for storing equipments, chemicals and glassware.

1. The working tables in science laboratory are provided with
   - **Sinks with Water Taps** For washing purposes and liquid waste disposal are provided on working table. Never throw any insoluble solid material like filter papers, broken glass apparatus into the sink as these can block the drain. Students should use taps only when required and should not waste any water. It is essential to clean the sinks regularly.
   - **Reagent Shelves** Reagents or chemicals to be used very frequently are kept on these shelves. Reagent bottles are arranged in a definite order on these shelves.
   - **Gas Taps** These are fitted on the working table for supply of LPG to the burners for heating purposes. A gas tap should be opened only when the gas is required for lighting the burner. Any leakage should be immediately brought to the notice of the teacher or other laboratory staff. Every laboratory is equipped with a few fire extinguishers fixed at convenient places.
2. The equipment and glassware of common use are stored separately in an almirah. These are generally issued to the students at the time of performing experiments.

3. The equipments like balances and microscopes are used less frequently, therefore, these are placed permanently at a fixed place. A physical balance (Fig. 1) is used for weighing powdered or solid materials (One must use weighing tubes or butter paper depending upon the nature of the material). The pan of the balance must be kept cleaned. The microscope (Fig. 2) must be placed near the window to ensure the availability of sufficient light needed.

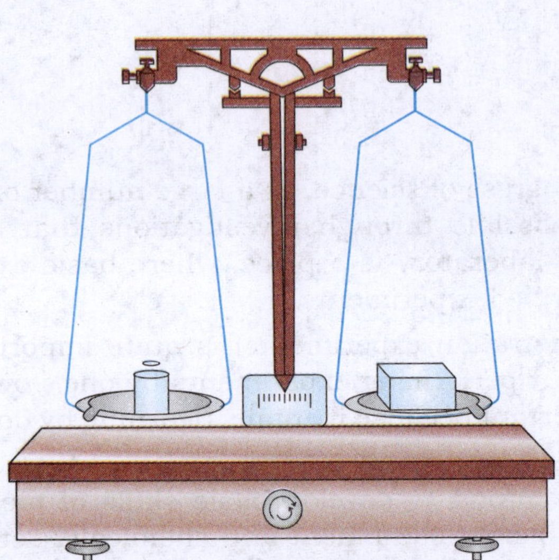
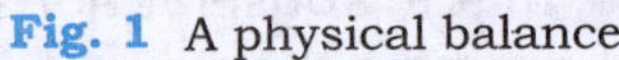

**Fig. 1** A physical balance

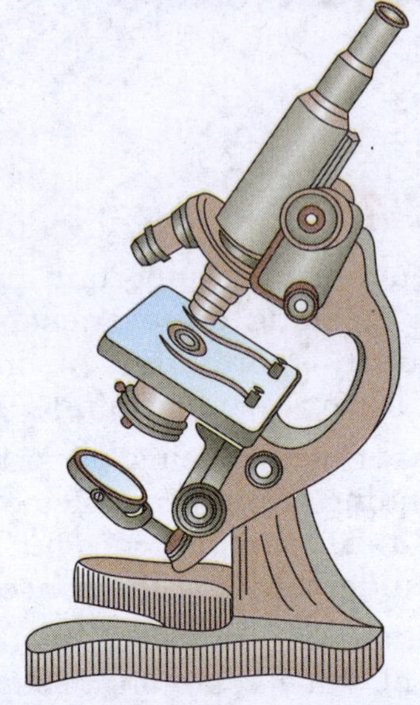

**Fig. 2** A compound microscope

4. Electrical connections are provided with all working tables for performing electricity and magnetism experiments.
5. A demonstration table is placed for teacher demonstration.
6. For the disposal of solid wastes, a dustbin may be provided either near each working table or at a common place in the laboratory.

Utility items like soldering rod, hammer, drill machine, pliers, hacksaw, cutter, screw drivers, etc. must be placed at a convenient place inside the laboratory.

## Safety Requirements in a Science Laboratory

A science laboratory should be equipped with the following safety requirements :

| | |
|---|---|
| **Exhaust Fans** | The laboratory should be well-ventilated and for this, exhaust fans must be fitted near the ceiling of laboratory for speedy removal of the waste gases to keep the laboratory free from polluted air. |
| **First Aid Box** | A first-aid must be readily available in science laboratory for use during accidents and emergencies. It is equipped with tincture of iodine, ferric chloride (alcoholic), burnol, savlon, cotton, sodium bicarbonate solution, adhesive plaster, bandages and scissors. |
| **Fire Extinguishers** | Every laboratory should be equipped with two or more fire extinguishers fixed at convenient places and science teacher/lab assistant should be well versed with its use. Sand or dry mud should also be available in laboratory. |
| **Eye Wash Fountain** | An eye wash fountain should be available in the laboratory. It is used in the case of irritation of eyes caused by chemicals and fumes. |

# Commonly Used Apparatus

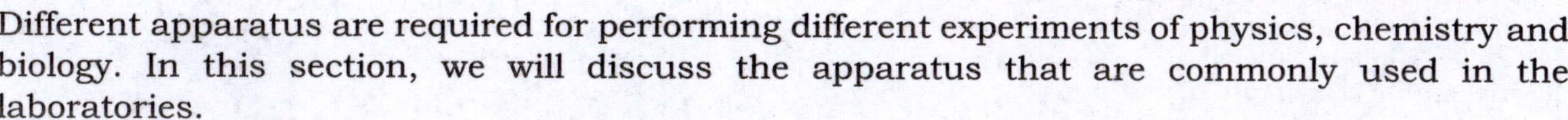

Different apparatus are required for performing different experiments of physics, chemistry and biology. In this section, we will discuss the apparatus that are commonly used in the laboratories.

## PHYSICS LABORATORY

Experiments performed in a physics laboratory are of a wide range. Different sets of apparatus are used for performing different experiments. Apparatus need to be handled carefully to retain their sensitivity. It is very essential to understand the sources of error for obtaining accurate results.
Some of the commonly used apparatus in physics laboratory are

| Name of the Apparatus | Use | Figures |
|---|---|---|
| **Spring Balance**<br>It is a type of weighing scale.<br>It has a hook on one end from where the object is suspended by a string. Reading is taken from the graduated brass plate present on the metallic case. | It is used to weigh various objects. | |
| **Meter Scale**<br>It is a straight strip made up of wood, metal or other material having a straight edge. It is graduated in centimetres and inches. | It is used to measure the length. | |
| **Stopclock**<br>It is a timing device similar to stop watch and often designed for measuring very brief time intervals. | It is used as a timer to measure the time of oscillations of pendulum. | |

| Name of the Apparatus | Use | Figures |
|---|---|---|
| **Galvanometer**<br>It is an instrument for detecting the existence of small currents and determining their strength. | It is a sensitive instrument used to detect the direct electric current. | 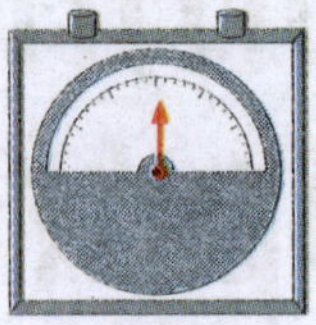 |
| **Ammeter**<br>A meter designed to measure the electric current is called ammeter. It is always connected in series within the circuit. | It is used to measure the current flowing in a circuit. |  |
| **Voltmeter**<br>A voltmeter is an instrument for measuring electrical potential difference between two points in an electric circuit. | It is used to measure the potential difference and is always connected in parallel within the circuit. |  |
| **Rheostat**<br>It is an adjustable resistor whose resistance may be changed without opening the circuit in which it is connected, thereby controlling the current in circuit. | It is used to vary current in the circuit. | 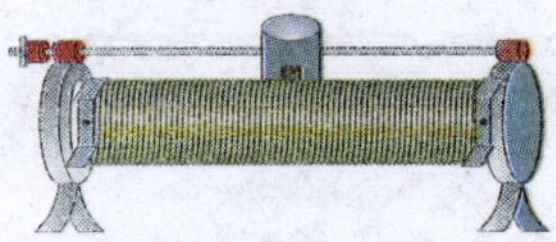 |
| **Concave Mirror**<br>A spherical mirror which is silvered from the outer curved side such that its reflecting surface is towards the inner side of the hollow sphere is called a concave mirror. | It is capable of reflecting all the parallel beams to the focus. |  |
| **Prism**<br>It is a block of glass or other transparent material enclosed by two inclined plane refracting surfaces at some fixed angle called "angle of prism". It has two triangular bases and three rectangular lateral surfaces which are inclined to one another. | It is capable of splitting the light into band of seven colours. | 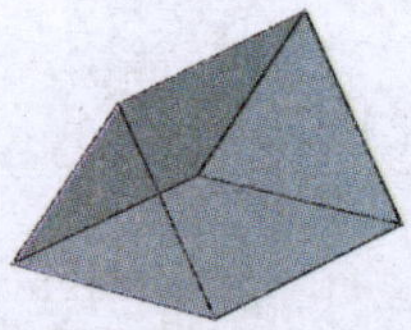 |
| **Convex Lens**<br>It is a converging lens with both surfaces convex in nature. It is thicker in middle and thinner at edges. | It is capable of converging all the light rays to the focus. |  |

# CHEMISTRY LABORATORY

Commonly used apparatus in a chemistry laboratory are

| Name of the Apparatus | Use | Figures |
|---|---|---|
| **Test Tubes**<br>These are the hollow glass tubes closed at one end and have a circular rim at the other. These are available in different diameter and lengths or different volumes. | These are used to carry out the chemical reactions. | |
| **Boiling Tube**<br>It is similar to the test tube but it is of larger diameter. | It is used for boiling or heating large volume of solution. | |
| **Test Tube Holder**<br>It contains an iron strip fitted in cylindrical wooden base. | It is used to hold the test tube containing liquids or solids during heating. | |
| **Test Tube Stand**<br>It is made up of plastic polypropylene. The holes in the top plate can hold the test tubes and its vertical pins for drying the tubes. | It is used for keeping the test tubes vertically. The cleaned test tubes are kept upside down to drain out water. | |
| **Test Tube Brush**<br>It is made up of thick hard iron wire with soft plastic bristles. | It is used for cleaning the test tube. | |
| **Beakers**<br>These are the cylindrical vessels with a large diameter and are usually made up of pyrex or corning glass. These are available in various sizes ranging from 5 mL to 2000 mL. | These are used for keeping the liquid solution during experimental work and to pour solution from one beaker to another. | |
| **Flasks** These are of three types:<br>(a) **Round Bottom Flask** It is round glass bottle flask and cannot be placed on the table directly due to its round bottom. | These are used for heating the contents. | |
| (b) **Flat Bottom Flask** It is a glass bottle having a flat bottom with a long narrow neck. It can be kept on the table without falling. | These are used for carrying out the chemical reactions and in distillation process. | |
| (c) **Conical Flask** It is a hollow glass vessel which is of conical shape and are available in various sizes ranging from 5 mL to 2000 mL, also referred as Erlen Meyer Flasks. | These are used for carrying out volumetric titrations. | |

| Name of the Apparatus | Use | Figures |
|---|---|---|
| **Funnel**<br>It is cone shaped hollow glass apparatus with a narrow long stem. These are available in various sizes. | It is used for filtration and transfer of liquids from one vessel to the other. They have diameter from 5-7 cm and may be made of plastic or glass. | |
| **Graduated or Measuring Cylinders**<br>It is a cylindrical shaped apparatus with graduated marking. It is made up of glass or plastic and is available in various volumes. | These are used for measuring volume of liquids and may be made of glass or plastic. These are available in sizes 10,25,50,100 and 250 mL. | 60<br>50<br>40<br>30<br>20<br>10 |
| **Iron Stand**<br>It is made of heavy cast iron base and a thick iron rod fitted on one side of the base. | Clamps and rings are fitted on the rod which is used to hold and separate the apparatus. | |
| **Wire Gauze**<br>A flat square piece of iron wire mesh in which asbestos paper is trapped at the centre of the gauze. | It is kept on the tripod stand to heat the beakers and flasks. | |
| **Mortar and Pestle**<br>It is a thick walled vessel with a hemispherical shape with a base. It is made up of porcelain. | It is used for grinding compounds and solid substances into fine powder with the help of pestle. | |
| **Water Bath**<br>It is a vessel made up of brass having oval shape. | It is filled with water and used for controlled heating or when direct heating of the flame is to be avoided. | |
| **China Dish or Evaporating Dish**<br>It is a hollow hemispherical shaped apparatus usually made up of porcelain. | It is used for evaporation and crystallisation purposes. | |
| **Watch Glass**<br>It is a small, circular piece of glassware. | It is used to dry and weigh the substances. | |
| **Glass Rod**<br>It is a thick cylindrical stick of glass which is not hollow and available in various thickness. | It is used for stirring and mixing of substances. | |

| Name of the Apparatus | Use | Figures |
|---|---|---|
| **Spatula**<br>It is made up of horn or plastic with a spoon like shape. | It is used like a spoon for handling small quantities of substances. | |
| **Tripod Stand**<br>It is made up of cast iron and possesses a triangular shape fitted with three rods acting as legs. | It is used to support the vessel to be heated. | |
| **Crucible Tongs**<br>It is made up of steel or iron. | It is used to hold hot beaker, China dish. | |
| **Bunsen Burner**<br>It is the most commonly used gas burner in school laboratories. | This apparatus is widely used in experiments that require heating. | |
| **Spirit Lamp**<br>A spirit lamp is like an ordinary lamp but this lamp uses spirit as a fuel. | In case Bunsen burner is not available in the laboratory, then spirit lamp can be used for heating. | |
| **Wash Bottle**<br>It is made up of plastic, polythene containing a thin tube. | It is used for washing and rinsing glass apparatus. | |

# BIOLOGY LABORATORY

The commonly used apparatus in biology laboratory are

| Name of the Apparatus | Use | Figures |
| --- | --- | --- |
| **Glass Slide**<br>It is a thin flat rectangular piece of glass. | A specimen is placed on the glass slide and seen under a microscope. | |
| **Magnifying Glass**<br>(Hand Lens)<br>It is a convex lens which is usually mounted in a frame with a handle. | It is used to produce a magnified image of an object. | |
| **Dropper**<br>It is usually a glass or soft plastic tubes tapered to a narrow point and fitted with a rubber bulb at the top. It is of various sizes. | It is used to add solutions in small quantities. | |
| **Petri Dish**<br>It is a shallow glass or plastic cylindrical shaped dish. | It is used for keeping small specimens. | |
| **Cover Slip**<br>It is a thin, flat piece of transparent material usually made of glass. It is typically square or rectangular, about 20 mm (4/5) wide and only a fraction of a millimetre thick. | It is placed over the specimen for viewing with a microscope. | |
| **Forceps**<br>These are hinged instrument. | These are used for grasping and holding objects. | |

## CLEANING OF GLASSWARE APPARATUS

For obtaining accurate and appropriate results, the glass and porcelain apparatus should be thoroughly cleaned before starting of an experiment.

- If the apparatus is very dirty and contaminated with dust and impurities like grease, then concentrated acids like $HNO_3$, HCl or chromic acid is used for cleaning. The apparatus is dipped in chromic acid solution for some time and then washed with excess of water.
- Sodium carbonate is used to clean beakers, flasks and China dish.
- Employ a suitable brush to clean the inner surface of burettes, test tubes, flask. Place the washed apparatus in an inverted position so that the water is drained off.

# How to Record an Experiment?

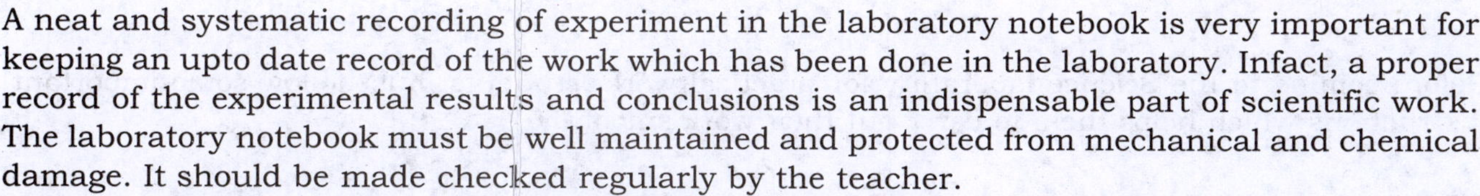

A neat and systematic recording of experiment in the laboratory notebook is very important for keeping an upto date record of the work which has been done in the laboratory. Infact, a proper record of the experimental results and conclusions is an indispensable part of scientific work. The laboratory notebook must be well maintained and protected from mechanical and chemical damage. It should be made checked regularly by the teacher.

## Sample Format to Record the Experiment

The experiment should be recorded in the laboratory notebook under the following heads as:

| Date...... | Experiment No. ...... | Page No. ...... |
|---|---|---|

**Aim** It should clearly state the objective of the experiment.

---

**Material Required** List all equipments, measuring devices and other items or materials to be used for performing the experiment.

---

**Theory** It must explain the basic principle(s), laws or theories on which the experiment is based. Wherever necessary, the mathematical law involved in the experiment should be supplemented with mathematical equations.

---

**Procedure** All the steps followed while carrying out the experiment should be mentioned in a proper sequence. Labelled diagrams, if any, should be drawn to present a pictorial view of the experimental set-up.

---

**Calculations/Observations** In case, calculations based on the observations are required to obtain the result of an experiment, correct formulae and units must be used while substituting the data. All calculations must be carried out carefully. The answer should be stated with proper SI units.

---

**Result** Clearly state the conclusions drawn from the experimental observations. If result depends upon the conditions of temperature and pressure, mention these conditions along with the result.

---

**Precautions** All the precautions taken while performing the experiment should be clearly mentioned. Although, some of the precautions taken during some experiments may be common, these usually change from one experiment to another depending on the nature of the experiment.

---

**Sources of Error** The possible sources of error that arise because of limitation of equipment, due to change in atmospheric conditions or any other reason, should also be stated.

These may include points for making the experiment more accurate and for better understanding of the basic principle involved.

# Lab Instructions

Before coming to the Science laboratory for practical work, students must follow some important instructions which helps them to carry out their work smoothly.

## Instructions to Perform Physics Experiments

To work efficiently in Physics laboratory, a student must follow the following instructions :

1. Before performing an experiment, the student should first thoroughly understand the theory of the experiment the objective of the experiment, the kind of apparatus needed and the procedure to be followed. The difficulties and doubts, if any, should be discussed with the teacher before hand.
2. The student should check up whether the right type of apparatus for the experiment to be performed is given to him or not.
3. Repeat every observation a number of times even though their values may be exactly the same each time. The student must bear in mind the proper plan for recording the observations. Recording in tabular form is essential in most of the experiments.
4. Wherever possible, the observations should be represented with the help of a graph.
5. Always mention the proper unit (if any) with the result.
6. **Accuracy** of a measuring instrument is considered as half of its least count. **Least count** is the smallest distance that any measuring instruments are able to measure. Measuring instruments that are used commonly in laboratory are scales, vernier callipers, screw gauge, spring balance, thermometer, analytical balance.
7. **Zero error** arises in a measuring instrument when its pointer, at its resting point, does not coincide with the zero mark on the scale. To obtain the accurate value, the zero error has to be added or subtracted from the reading taken after measurement.
8. **Error due to friction** may arise if movement of an object over another surface is involved. Hence, error due to friction should be minimised.
   For example, in a spring balance, the strip carrying the pointer should be lubricated and tapped gently before the use otherwise errors due to friction arises which would affect the result.
9. **Error due to suspension** can arise if the support from which an object is suspended moves during the oscillation of the suspended object i.e. in the case of a simple pendulum. To avoid this error, the support should be rigid, so that time period can be measured accurately.
10. **Error due to spilling** arises when a solid or liquid is added to another liquid readily in a hurry. To avoid this type of error carefully and gently transfer the liquids (or solid).
11. **Error of parallax** should be avoided by placing your eye at right angle to the plane of the scale and vertically above the point to be read.
12. **Percentage error** between 5% to 10% for recording observations and calculation of result is allowed.
13. The degree of accuracy of measurement of each quantity should always be kept in mind so that the final result does not show any fictious accuracy. The result obtained should be suitably rounded off.

# Instructions to Perform Chemistry Experiments

To work efficiently in Chemistry laboratory, a student must follow the following instructions :

1. After the instructions given by the teacher, collect the apparatus from the laboratory assistant in queue.
2. Before starting an experiment, check all your apparatus carefully to make sure that they are in good condition. Do not use any cracked apparatus.
3. Thoroughly clean the apparatus to be used.
4. Do only the experiments assigned, unallotted experiments should not be done.
5. All the experiments must be conducted under the supervision of qualified teachers only.
6. Do your experiment honestly without caring for the final result. Record the observations on a rough note-book instead of writing on the pieces of paper.
7. Plan your work, so that it is finished in the stipulated time.
8. Keep your seat clean. If an acid or other corrosive chemical is spilled, wash it off with water.
9. Always wear goggles to protect your eyes.
10. Wear closed-toe shoes to protect the feet from chemical spills and sharp objects.
11. Do not eat or drink in the laboratory.
12. Wash your hands thoroughly with soap after performing the experiment.
13. Switch off gas burners when they are not in use.
14. Solid waste materials like filter paper and test tube should be thrown only in the dustbin and not in the sink.
15. After the experiment, clean all the apparatus and return it to the laboratory assistant.
16. Dispose all waste liquids in the sink and allow water to run for some time by opening the water tap.
17. Never dilute an acid by adding water to the concentrated acids because it is an exothermic reaction and the liquid may bump out. Always dilute the acid by slowly adding acid to water with stirring.

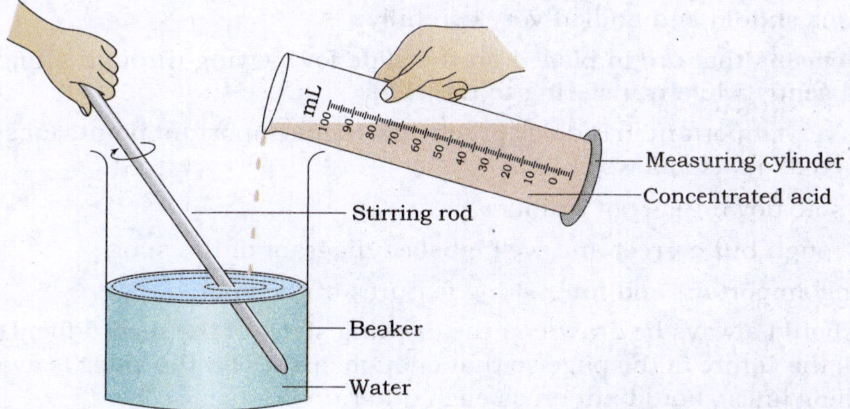


Fig. 3 Correct way of adding acid to water for dilution

# Instructions to Perform Biology Experiments

Before coming to the Biology laboratory for practical work, students must be acquainted with certain basic rules of the laboratory. This enables them to do their practicals smoothly, effectively and efficiently.

Some important instructions for the students are discussed below :

1. A student must carry the following things to the laboratory for every practical session to perform various type of experiments.
   - Laboratory notebook
   - Laboratory manual
   - Auxillary (or rough) notebook
   - A pencil
   - Eraser
   - Scale
   - Dissection box.

**Note** Dissection box should contain a pair of small forceps, a pair of large forceps, a pair of small and large scissors, a fine blade or razor for section cutting, needles (two), brush (No. 00) and a magnifying glass.

2. Handle the microscope carefully. It should always be placed on a stable table.
3. Always keep the microscope in upright position by holding it with both the hands. Do not swing the microscope with one hand while carrying it as the loosely fixed lens may fall.
4. Always clean the lens mirror and stage of the microscope properly before use.
5. Do not touch the lens or mirror as fingerprints may spoil the image.
6. Do not lower the lens too much, as it may touch the specimen or water.
7. While **studying slides** under the microscope, do not disturb the slide focussed by the teacher. In case you face any difficulty, seek the help of your teacher. You can move the fine adjustment screw to bring the slide in sharp focus.
8. For **studying the museum specimens**, the following steps need to be followed :
   - Carefully study the characteristics of the specimen from the book.
   - Try to find out these characteristics in the specimen.
   - Draw a line diagram of the specimen. If needed, draw more than one view of the specimen.
   - Always write classification for the entire specimen.
   - Specimens should be handled very carefully.
   - The specimens that are to placed on the slide for viewing through a microscope should be handled gently while transfering to the slide.
9. **Spotting** is very important in Biology practicals. Some important points for spotting that should be remembered are as follows :
   - Always note down the spot number.
   - Draw a rough but correct and well labelled diagram of the spot.
   - Write only important and interesting features of the spot.
10. Diagrams should always be drawn on the drawing sheet of the record file. Draw large and neat diagrams in the centre of the page so that enough spaces on the sides is available for labelling. While labelling lines should not cross each other.

## General Lab Instruction

1. Always carry practical record book, laboratory manual, notebook (to record observations), pen, pencil, scale, eraser, sharpener, scissors, forceps, scalpel, dissecting needle, brush, blades, etc. to the laboratory.
2. Maintain discipline and silence in the lab.
3. Replace all laboratory equipment to its assigned place in the laboratory once the practical work is over.
4. Follow the instructions given by the teacher attentively.
5. Perform the experiment carefully and note down the observations.
6. Do not manipulate your results in any circumstances.
7. Use newspaper or blotting paper while using stains so as not to spoil the table.
8. Draw the diagrams neatly and label them correctly. Use fine HB pencil while drawing.
9. Do not play, whistle or stoop into your partner's set-up.
10. Be familiar with the handling of first aid kit and fire extinguisher. In case of any accident or injury or breakage of apparatus, report to the teacher immediately.
11. Students must prepare in advance for the experiment, they will perform in the laboratory.
12. Students must be punctual and should not be absent from their practical class and should reach the laboratory as soon as the period starts. This will enable to keep their practical work upto date.
13. All equipments such as microscope, physical balance, measuring items and glassware must be handled with care. Carelessness will not only damage the instrument or apparatus but may also cause injury to the students.

# Safety Precautions

To avoid unnecessary risk or injury during laboratory work, the students are advised to observe some general and safety precautions. Here, we will discuss all the precautions that are need to be observe in Physics, Chemistry and Biology laboratory.

## Physics Laboratory

Although in Physics laboratory many chemicals are not used still there are chances for accidents to occur. In order to avoid such accidents, we need to follows some safety precautions :

1. Handle the objects carefully and cautiously especially those made of glass to avoid any damage.
2. Use gloves while handling hot objects and always test the temperature of an object before picking it up.
3. Always pay proper attention while loosening or tightening screws and bolts as some of them may break easily.

### Precautions while Performing Experiments with Electricity

While performing the experiments with electricity some safety precautions should be observed :

1. Do not touch the live wire directly.
2. While making connections, the circuit diagram should be followed carefully. Take the polarity of the terminals of the battery, ammeter, voltmeter into consideration while making the connections.
3. The power switch should be turned off and the connections should be removed on finishing an experiment involving electricity.

## Chemistry Laboratory

The following safety precautions will enable us to perform experiments in a more secure way.

1. **Handling of Glass Apparatus**
   (i) Hot apparatus should not be placed on working table directly because it may spoil the working table. Place it on a glazed tile or a wire gauze.
   (ii) Be careful with glass equipment, while inserting a glass rod or tube or thermometer through a rubber cork, lubricate the glass and protect your hands with a cloth towel and use a gentle twisting motion.

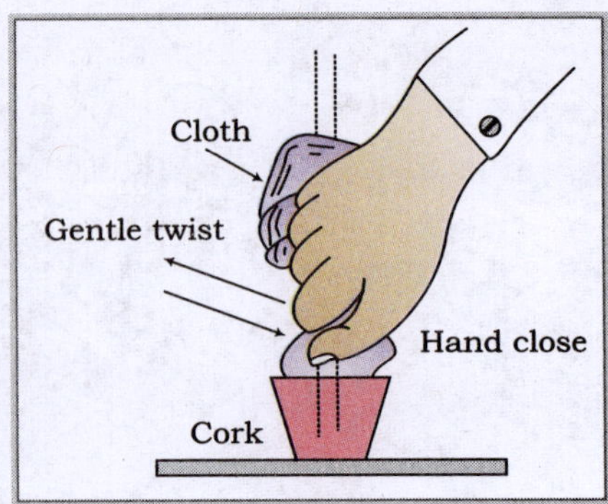


Fig. 4 Correct way of inserting a glass tube in a cork

2. **Handling Chemicals**

(i) Do not touch or taste or smell any chemical with your bare hands as it may be corrosive and poisonous.

(ii) Before using a reagent bottle, read the label very carefully to be sure that you are using the correct reagent.

(iii) Always keep reagent bottles securely closed and labelled.

(iv) Replace reagents to their original positions after use.

(v) Never pour partially used reagents back into the reagent bottle.

(vi) Be economical with reagents and chemicals, only small quantities need to be used.

3. **While Heating the Apparatus**

(i) Take proper care while heating the test tube. Never heat the contents of test tube by pointing towards your face. Hold it at an angle of 45° away from your face.

(ii) For smelling the vapours, fan the vapours gently with your hands towards the nose. Avoid direct smelling of vapours.

(iii) Heat the test tube gently and uniformly. Move the test tube in and out of the flame to allow time for heat transfer.

(iv) Heat the area near the surface of the test tube slightly more than the base of the tube. This concentrates boiling near the surface of the liquid and reduces the potential for bumping and boil over.

(v) Do not heat any flammable liquids like alcohol directly on flame.

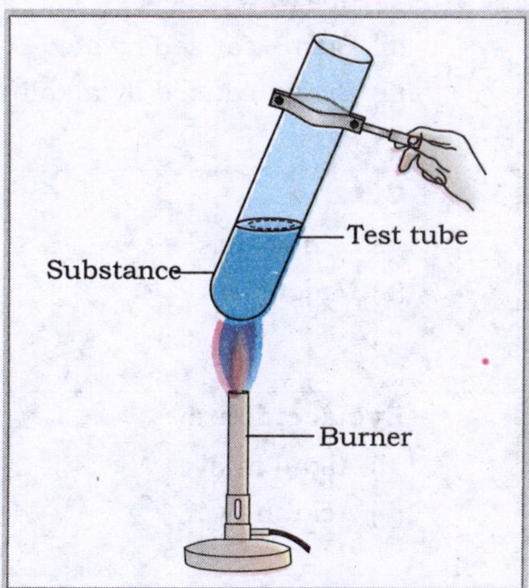


**Fig. 5** Proper heating

## Biology Laboratory

In Biology laboratory, following safety precautions are need to be observed :

1. Care should be taken while handling of all dissection instruments like razor, blade etc.
2. Do not use excessive force when working with sharp instruments.
3. All needles and syringes, razor blades and other sharp items need to be disposed of in a sharp container.
4. Do not touch broken glass with bare hands.
5. Never use fingers to hold a part of the specimen while cutting.
6. Gloves should be worn while handling the stains.

## FIRST AID TREATMENT

A first aid kit is an important part of a science laboratory which is placed at an easily accessible place. Accidents in the laboratory are often occur due to the carelessness or lack of attention. Most of the accidents take place due to improper handling of chemicals and apparatus.

In case, if it happens, first aid treatment must be provided immediately. The victim should be taken to the doctor, if required. The probable accidents, injuries and their first aid emergency treatments are listed below :

| | Type of accident | First aid treatment |
|---|---|---|
| 1. | **Burns** | |
| | (i) Burns caused by steam or hot water | • Wash the affected part with cold water, cool and dry it with clean cloth and apply burnol. |
| | (ii) Burns caused by acid | • Wash the wounded part with water and apply a dilute solution of sodium hydrogen carbonate. |
| | (iii) Burns caused by alkali | • Wash with ample of water to remove alkali and then wash with dilute acetic acid. |
| 2. | **Cuts** | |
| | (i) Minor cuts | • Allow to bleed for a few seconds. Remove the glass piece if any. Apply methylated spirit and cover it with a piece of cotton or you can apply $FeCl_3$ solution to stop bleeding. |
| | (ii) Major cuts | • Apply pressure above the cut to stop bleeding. Call the doctor immediately. |
| 3. | **Eye accidents** | |
| | (i) Alkali in eye | • Wash thoroughly with water and then with 1% boric acid solution. |
| | (ii) Acid in eye | • Wash thoroughly with water, afterwards with 1% sodium bicarbonate solution and then with water again. |
| 4. | **Poisons** | |
| | (i) Poisons not swallowed | • Spit out immediately. Wash mouth with plenty of water. |
| | (ii) Inhalation of gases like $Cl_2$, $SO_2$, $Br_2$, etc., causing suffocation | • Loosen the clothes at the neck. At once go in the open air. Inhale dilute vapours of ammonia or gargle with sodium bicarbonate solution. |
| | (iii) Acid swallowed | • Drink lot of water. Drink lime water. No emetic should be taken. |
| | (iv) Caustic alkalies swallowed | • Drink plenty of water. Drink a glass of lemon or orange juice. No emetic should be taken. |
| 5. | **Fire** | |
| | (i) Beaker containing inflammable liquid catches fire | • Immediately cover the beaker with duster or damp cloth. |
| | (ii) Clothes catch fire | • Do not run in haste. Wrap with a blanket, then lie down on the floor and roll. |

**Go to the doctor after getting first aid.**

# Experiment 1 (a)

## AIM

Preparation of true solution of common salt, sugar and alum.

## Materials Required

Powder samples of common salt [sodium chloride (NaCl)], sugar [sucrose ($C_{12}H_{22}O_{11}$)], crushed alum [potassium aluminium sulphate, $[K_2SO_4 \cdot Al_2(SO_4)_3 \cdot 24H_2O]$, distilled water, boiling tubes, pipette, test tube stand, spatula and glass rod.

## Theory/Principle

A true **solution** is a **homogeneous** mixture of two or more substances. In a solution, there is a homogeneity at the particle level, i.e. particles are evenly distributed. A solution has a **solvent** (component present in large quantity) and a **solute** (component present in small quantity) as its two components. When small amount of a solid (solute) such as common salt, sugar and alum is added to water (solvent) and stirred, a homogeneous mixture is obtained, which is transparent and stable.

In a **true solution**, the size of solute particles is very small less than 1 nanometer ($1 nm = 10^{-9}$ m or $10^{-7}$ cm) that they cannot be seen even with a microscope and thus, cannot be separated by the method of filtration. A ture solution does not scatter light and light can easily pass through it. These solutions do not show Tyndall effect (scattering of light by colloids)and they also do not exhibit Brownian motion. They are highly stable, i.e. solute particles do not settle down, e.g. *aq.* $C_2H_5OH$, *aq.* NaCl, *aq.* $FeSO_4$.

## Procedure

### 1. To Prepare True Solution of Common Salt

- Take a clean boiling tube.
- Pour 30 mL of distilled water in it, with the help of a pipette.
- Add about 1 g of common salt in boiling tube with the help of a spatula.
- With the help of a glass rod, stir the mixture for sometime.
- Allow the boiling tube to stand for 5-6 minutes. This solution should not be disturbed during the standing time.
- Observe and record whether the mixture formed is homogeneous or heterogeneous.

The process of preparing a true solution of common salt is shown in Fig. 1.

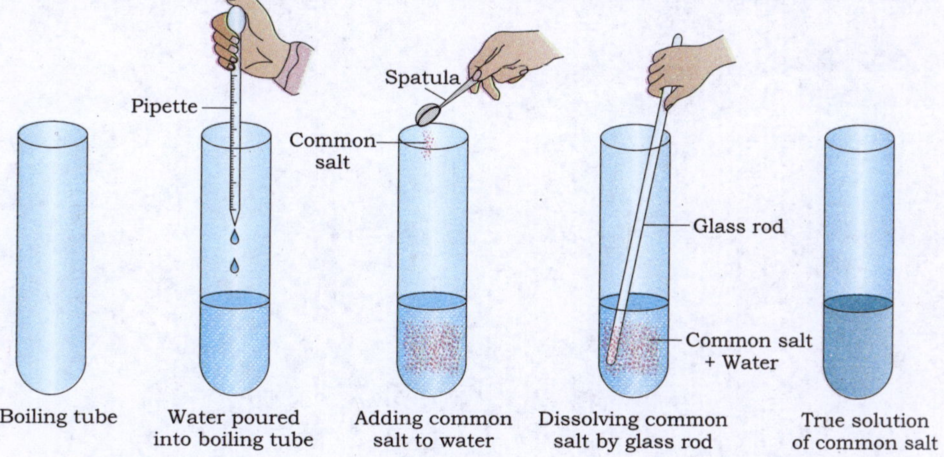


**Fig. 1** Process of preparing a true solution of common salt

## Observation

1 g of common salt dissolves completely in 30 mL of distilled water at a particular condition, i.e., temperature and pressure. The solution thus obtained is transparent and particles do not settle down even after keeping the solution undisturbed for sometime.

### 2. To Prepare True Solution of Sugar

- Take a clean boiling tube.
- Pour 30 mL of distilled water in it, with the help of a pipette.
- Add about 1 g of sugar in boiling tube with the help of a spatula.
- With the help of a glass rod, stir the mixture for some time.
- Allow the boiling tube to stand for 5-6 minutes. This solution should not be disturbed during the standing time.
- Observe and record whether the mixture formed is homogeneous or heterogeneous.

The process of preparing a true solution of sugar is shown in Fig. 2.

**Fig. 2** Process of preparing a true solution of sugar

## Observation

1 g of sugar dissolves completely in 30 mL of distilled water at a particular condition, i.e, temperature and pressure. The solution thus obtained is transparent and particles do not settle down even after keeping the solution undisturbed for sometime.

## 3. To Prepare True Solution of Alum

- Take a clean boiling tube.
- Pour 30 mL of distilled water in it, with the help of a pipette.
- Add about 1 g of crushed alum in boiling tube with the help of a spatula.
- With the help of a glass rod, stir the mixture for some time.
- Allow the boiling tube to stand for 5-6 minutes. This solution should not be disturbed during the standing time.
- Observe and record whether the mixture formed is homogeneous or heterogeneous

The process of preparing a true solution of alum is shown in Fig. 3.

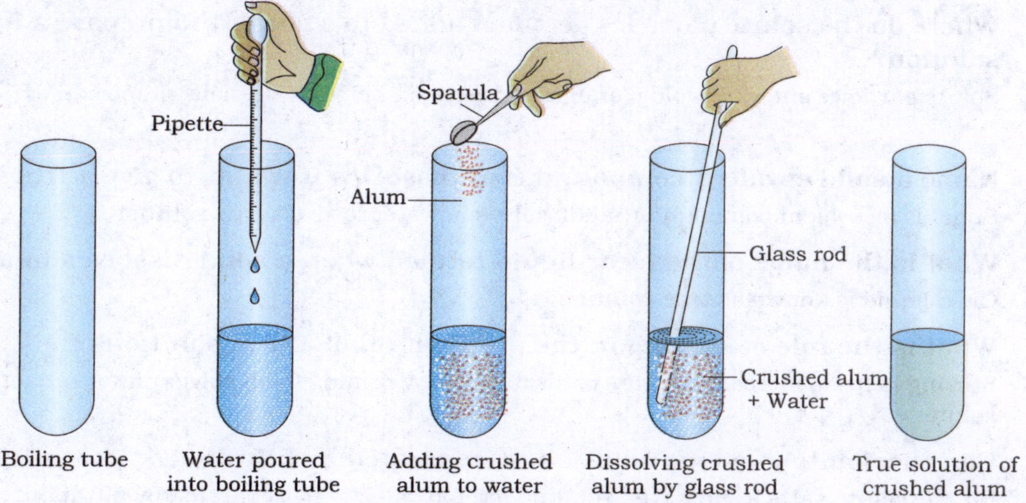


**Fig. 3** Process of preparing a true solution of alum

## Observation

1 g of crushed alum dissolves completely in 30 mL of distilled water at a particular condition, i.e. temperature and pressure. The solution thus obtained is transparent and particles do not settle down on keeping the solution undisturbed for some time.

## Result

In all the three cases, a clear and transparent solutions are obtained which shows that they form a true solution which are homogeneous and very stable in nature.

### PRECAUTIONS

1. *Take the powdered form of solid solute so that it dissolves easily in water.*
2. *Stir the contents thoroughly until all the solutes (salt, sugar and alum) dissolves completely.*
3. *The ends of the glass rod should be smooth so that it does not break the test tube while stirring.*
4. *Clean the spatula before use, everytime.*
5. *Clean the glass rod properly before every use.*

## Suggested Experiments

1. Prepare a true solution of vinegar in water and study its properties.
2. Prepare a true solution of carbon dioxide gas in soda water (it is a gas in liquid type of solution) and study its properties.

## Viva-Voce

**Q. 1 What is a true solution?**

**Ans.** A homogeneous mixture in which the size of the particles is less than 1nm ($10^{-9}$ m or $10^{-7}$ cm) and whose particles are not visible to the naked eye is called a true solution.

**Q. 2 Give two examples of a true solution.**

**Ans.** Solution of common salt in water and sugar in water.

**Q. 3 Where do the solute particles go when added to a solvent to prepare a true solution?**

**Ans.** Solute particles enter the voids (or empty spaces) in between the solvent molecules.

**Q. 4 Name a solid covalent compound that dissolves in water to give a true solution.**

**Ans.** Sugar is a covalent compound that dissolves in water to give a true solution.

**Q. 5 What is the name of the clear liquid formed when a solid dissolves in a liquid?**

**Ans.** Clear liquid is known as true solution.

**Q. 6 What is the role of stirring in the preparation of a true solutions?**

**Ans.** Stirring helps to increase the rate of dissolution by brining fresh solvent into contact with the solute.

**Q. 7 Can the solute in a true solution be separated by filtration?**

**Ans.** No, the solute particles in a true solution are too small to be separated by filtration.

**Q. 8 What would happen if the solute is added in excess?**

**Ans.** If the solute is added in excess, it will not dissolve completely, and the solution will become saturated.

## Questions From NCERT Lab Manual

**Q. 1 Why are the particles of a true solution not visible to naked eye?**

**Ans.** The particles of a true solution are not visible to the naked eye as they are very small in size, i.e. less than 1 nm ($1 \text{ nm} = \frac{1}{10^9} \text{ m} = 10^{-9} \text{ m}$).

**Q. 2 What will be your observation, when a beam of light is passed through a true solution?**

**Ans.** A beam of light is passed straight through a true solution. The path does not get illuminated that means it does not exhibit Tyndall effect.

# Experiment 1 (b)

## AIM

Preparation of a suspension of soil, chalk powder and fine sand in water.

## Materials Required

Three boiling tubes (bigger in size), test tube stand, glass rod, a spatula, measuring pipette or measuring cylinder, small sample of soil, chalk powder, fine sand and clean water.

## Theory/Principle

A **suspension** is a heterogeneous mixture of two or more substances. In suspension, the solute particles do not dissolve but remain suspended throughout the bulk of the medium. These particles are visible to the naked eye.

The particle size is greater than 1000 nm ($10^{-6}$ m). Rays of light cannot pass through suspension. On allowing the suspension to stand for a while, the particles of the solute settle down due to effect of gravity. Hence, a suspension is unstable in nature.

Some common examples of a suspension are paint dyes suspended in turpentine oil, muddy water etc.

## Procedure

### 1. To Prepare Suspension of Soil

- Take a clean boiling tube.
- Pour 30 mL of distilled water in it, with the help of a pipette.
- Add about 1 g of soil in boiling tube with the help of a spatula.
- With the help of a glass rod, stir the mixture for some time.
- Allow the boiling tube to stand for 5-6 minutes. This solution should not be disturbed during the standing time.
- Observe and record whether the mixture formed is homogeneous or heterogeneous.

The process of preparing a suspension of soil is shown in [Fig. 1.]

**Fig. 1** Process of preparing a suspension of soil

## Observation

Soil particles in boiling tube are clearly visible and they remain suspended and finally settle down at the bottom of the boiling tube.

### 2. To Prepare Suspension of Chalk Powder

- Take a clean boiling tube.
- Pour 30 mL of distilled water in it, with the help of a pipette.
- Add about 1 g of chalk powder in boiling tube with the help of a spatula.
- With the help of a glass rod, stir the mixture for sometime.
- Allow the boiling tube to stand for 5-6 minutes. This solution should not be disturbed during the standing time.
- Observe and record whether the mixture formed is homogeneous or heterogeneous.

The process of preparing a suspension of chalk powder in water is shown in Fig. 2.

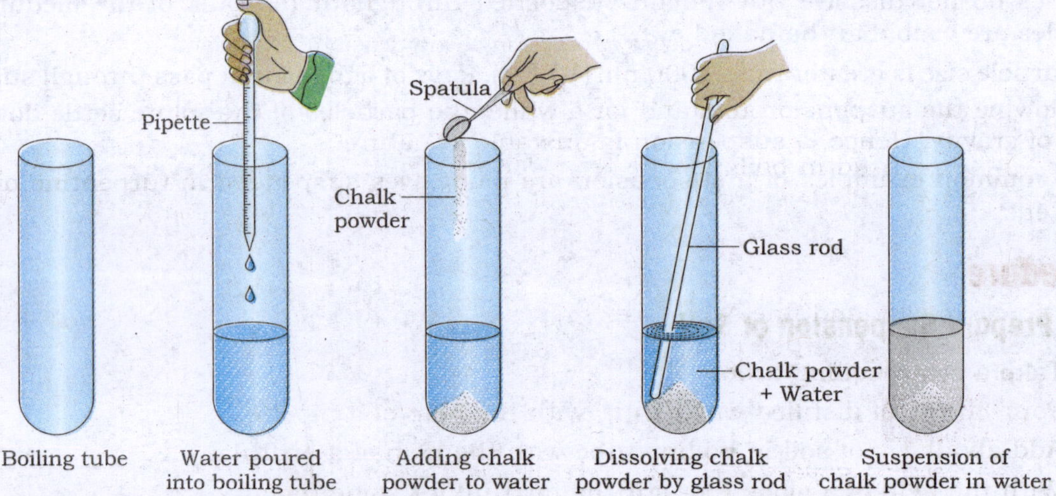


**Fig. 2** Process of preparing a suspension of chalk powder

## Observation

Particles of chalk powder in boiling tube are clearly visible. They remain suspended and finally settle down at the bottom of the tube.

### 3. To Prepare Suspension of Fine Sand

- Take a clean boiling tube.
- Pour 30 mL of distilled water in it, with the help of a pipette.
- Add about 1 g of fine sand in boiling tube with the help of a spatula.
- With the help of a glass rod, stir the mixture for sometime.
- Allow the boiling tube to stand for 5-6 minutes. This solution should not be disturbed during the standing time.
- Observe and record whether the mixture formed is homogeneous or heterogeneous.

The process of preparing a suspension of fine sand in water is shown in Fig. 3.

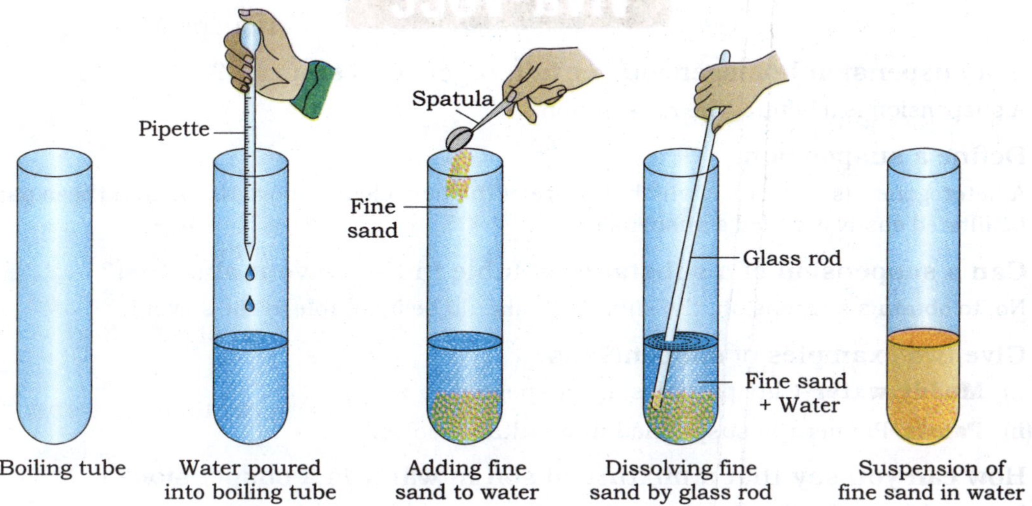


**Fig. 3** Process of preparing a suspension of fine sand

## Observation

Particles of fine sand in boiling tube are clearly visible and remains suspended for sometime. These particles settle down at the bottom of the boiling tube.

## Result

Soil, chalk powder and fine sand form suspension in water which are heterogeneous in which small solid particles settled down at the bottom of the boiling tube.

### PRECAUTIONS

1. *While preparing suspension of chalk, take the fine powder of chalk.*
2. *While preparing suspension of fine sand in water, sieve the ordinary sand through muslin cloth so as to obtain fine sand.*
3. *Stir the contents of the test tube thoroughly to make a proper suspension.*
4. *Use clean glassware to avoid contamination.*
5. *Do not inhale fine powders (like chalk).*

## Suggested Experiments

1. Prepare a suspension of milk of magnesia in water and study its properties.
2. Prepare a solution of common salt in water and a solution of sand in water then differentiate between their properties.

## Viva-Voce

**Q. 1 Is a suspension homogeneous or heterogeneous solution?**

**Ans.** A suspension is a heterogeneous solution.

**Q. 2 Define a suspension.**

**Ans.** A heterogeneous mixture in which the size of the particles is above $10^{-6}$ m and these particles can be filtered easily is called a suspension.

**Q. 3 Can a suspension of a substance soluble in the solvent obtained?**

**Ans.** No, to obtain a suspension, the substance should be insoluble in the solvent.

**Q. 4 Give two examples of suspensions.**

**Ans** (i) **Muddy water** Clay particles are dispersed in water.

(ii) **Paints** Pigment is suspended in a suitable solvent.

**Q. 5 How can you say that a mixture of soil in water is a suspension?**

**Ans.** In the mixture of soil and water, soil particles remain suspended in the solution are seen by naked eye.

**Q. 6 What is the size of the particle in any suspension?**

**Ans.** In any suspension, the particle size is larger than $10^{-6}$ m.

**Q. 7 Which of the following show sedimentation–true solution or suspension?**

**Ans.** Suspension shows sedimentation.

**Q. 8 Write two properties of a suspension.**

**Ans.** (i) A suspension is a heterogeneous mixture.

(ii) A suspension scatters a beam of light passing through it due to the presence of large particles.

**Q. 9 Four students were asked to add chalk powder, milk, sand and soil in water. They were asked in which sample, there is no suspension formed when water is added to them?**

**Ans.** Milk is a colloidal solution and not suspension.

**Q.10 Four students were asked to add chalk powder, common salt, oil and milk to beakers *A*, *B*, *C* and *D* containing water. On stirring the content, in which beaker suspension would be obtained?**

**Ans.** By dissolving chalk powder in water (i.e., Beaker *A*) suspension would be obtained.

## Questions From NCERT Lab Manual

**Q. 1 What is the order of the size of a particle that can be seen by naked eyes?**

**Ans.** The size of particles that can be seen by naked eye are of the order of $10^{-6}$ m or more.

**Q. 2 What will be your observation when a beam of light is passed through a suspension?**

**Ans.** When a beam of light is passed through a suspension, it gets scattered (because its particles are quite large).

# Experiment 1 (c)

## AIM

Preparation of a colloidal solution of starch in water and egg albumin/milk in water.

## Materials Required

Three clean beakers each of 100 mL capacity, a watch glass, a glass rod, starch powder, egg albumin milk (preferably raw or full-fat), distilled water, bunsen burner, wire gauze and tripod stand.

## Theory/Principle

A **colloid** is a heterogeneous mixture, consisting of two or more substances. The particles of a colloid are uniformly spread throughout the solution. Due to the relatively smaller size of particles as compared to that of a suspension, the mixture appears to be homogeneous. But actually, a colloidal solution is a heterogeneous mixture.

The size of the particles of solute in a colloid is from 1 to 1000 nm ($10^{-7}$ to $10^{-4}$ cm) in diameter. Because of the small size of colloidal particles, we cannot see them with naked eye.

When a small amount of starch or egg albumin is added to the water and stirred well, the solid particles get dispersed in water such that medium is homogeneous but cloudy in appearance.

## Procedure

### 1. Preparation of Colloidal Solution of Starch in Water

- Take about 30 mL of distilled water in a beaker (100 mL capacity) and heat it upto about 50°C for about 5 minutes. Try to maintain the temperature of water around 50°C.
- Take 1 g of starch in a watch glass and add a few drops of cold water to make a thin paste.

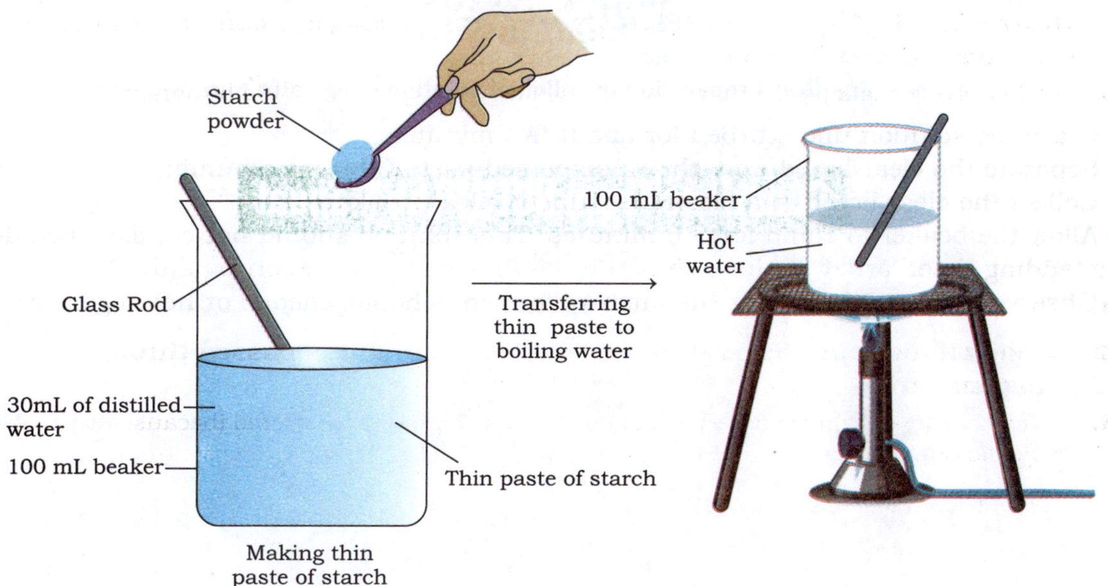


**Fig. 1** Preparation of colloidal solution of starch

- Transfer the paste of starch to the boiling water with continuous stirring so that no lump formation takes place.
- Stir the contents thoroughly till the paste of starch disappears [Fig. 1].
- Heat the mixture of starch and water for about 10 minutes.
- If there are suspended particles (lumps) separate them by filtration.
- Collect the filtrate in a clean beaker.
- Allow the beaker to stand for 5-6 minutes. This solution should not be disturbed during standing time.
- Observe and record whether the mixture formed is homogeneous or heterogeneous.

## Observation

**After adding paste to the boiling water, initially a white turbid solution can be seen which become almost transparent on boiling. Further on keeping solution undisturbed for sometime, it becomes translucent.**

## 2. Preparation of Colloidal Solution of Egg Albumin/Milk in Water

- Take about 30 mL of distilled water in a clean beaker (100 mL capacity) and heat it upto about 35°C (if required).
- Break an egg and remove the egg shells.
- Separate yellow part of the egg material yolk from the white portion (egg albumin).
- Add a very small quantity of egg albumin to warm water (Powder of egg albumin if available may also be used in place of fresh sample).
- With the help of a spoon, add more albumin and stir the contents thoroughly [Fig. 2(a)].

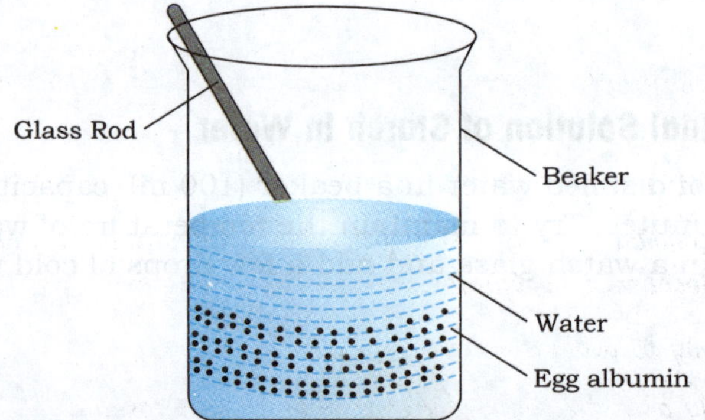


**Fig. 2(a)** Preparation of colloidal solution of egg albumin

- Leave the solution undisturbed for about five minutes.
- Separate the clear liquid from the undispersed part of the egg albumin.
- Collect the clear liquid in a clean test tube or clean beaker.
- Allow the beaker to stand for 5-6 minutes. This solution should not be disturbed during standing time.
- Observe and record whether the mixture formed is homogeneous or heterogeneous.

- Similarly, to prepare colloidal solution of milk, add about 50 mL of fresh milk to water and stir it with the help of a glass rod [Fig. 2(b)].

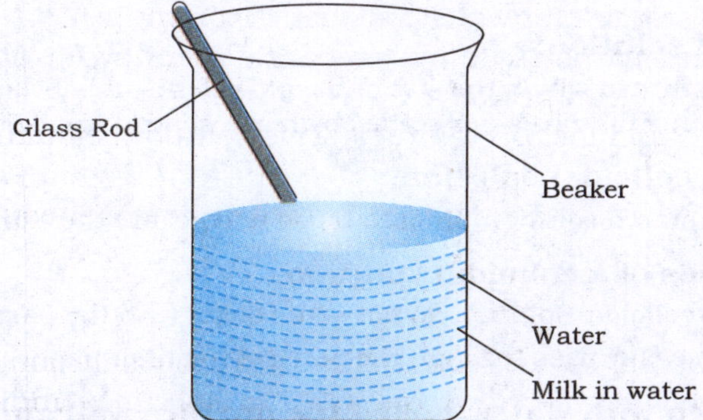


**Fig. 2 (b)** Preparation of colloidal solution of milk in water

## Observation

I. Egg albumin forms a turbid colloidal solution which is translucent in nature.

II. Milk forms a opaque colloidal solution.

## Result

Colloidal solutions of starch in water and egg albumin/milk in water are obtained which are heterogeneous.

### PRECAUTIONS

1. While adding starch slurry into warm water, stirring must be continued so that no lump formation takes place.
2. Dry starch should never be added to warm water to prevent lump formation.
3. While preparing the colloidal solution of egg albumin, temperature of water should be controlled (≈ 35°C) properly. Because it coagulates at high temperatures.
4. Use distilled water only to avoid ion contamination.
5. Add substances slowly and stir continuously to maintain uniformity.
6. Use proper lighting to observe transparency and Tyndall effect.
7. Handle the filtration setup carefully.

## Suggested Experiments

1. Prepare a colloidal solution of blue ink in water and study its properties.
2. Prepare a sugar solution and soap solution and observe which of the two will scatter light.

## Viva-Voce

**Q. 1 Define a colloidal solution.**

**Ans.** A heterogeneous mixture in which the size of the particles is in between $10^{-7}$cm to $10^{-4}$ cm, such that the particle neither dissolves nor settle down in a solvent is called a colloidal solution.

**Q. 2 Give examples of colloidal solution.**

**Ans.** Soap solution, milk, starch solution, human blood and gel are the examples of colloidal solution.

**Q. 3 Give two properties of a colloidal solution.**

**Ans.** (i) The particles of a colloidal solution do not settle down with the passage of time.

(ii) Colloidal solution easily pass through the pores of the filter paper.

**Q. 4 Rohit mixed starch with water, boiled the mixture well and stirred it. What did he observe?**

**Ans.** Rohit observed that starch forms a translucent mixture with water.

**Q. 5 A student was asked to mix the white part of an egg albumin in water and stir well. What type of solution is obtained?**

**Ans.** A translucent solution is obtained by mixing white part of an egg albumin in water.

**Q. 6 Name one colloidal solution where both the dispersed phase and the dispersion medium are liquids.**

**Ans.** A colloidal solution of milk in water.

**Q. 7 What are the two components of a colloidal solution called?**

**Ans.** The two components of a colloidal solution are called dispersion medium and dispersed phase.

**Q. 8 Give a technique through which colloids can be separated?**

**Ans.** Colloids can be separated by method of centrifugation.

**Q. 9 What is a gel?**

**Ans.** A gel is a colloid in which dispersion medium is a solid and dispersed phase is a liquid.

## Questions From NCERT Lab Manual

**Q. 1 What is the difference in the particle size of colloid, true solution and suspension?**

**Ans.** The size of particles in a colloid is in between 1 nm and 1000 nm in diameter (1 nm $=10^{-9}$ m).

In a true solution, it is less than 1nm in diameter.

In a suspension, it is larger than 1000 nm in diameter.

Thus, the particle's size follows the order : suspension > colloidal solution > true solution.

**Q. 2 What will be the effect of passing light through colloidal solution of sulphur?**

**Ans.** When a beam of light is passed through a colloidal solution of sulphur, the light gets scattered by the sulphur particles. As a result, the path of the light gets illuminated. It shows Tyndall effect.

# Experiment 1 (d)

## AIM

To distinguish between a true solution, a suspension and a colloidal solution on the basis of transparency, filtration criterion and stability.

## Materials Required

Three test tubes, funnel, filter paper, test tube stand, solution of common salt, solution of egg albumin and solution of chalk powder (already prepared).

## Theory/Principle

**True solutions** are transparent and its components cannot be separated by filtration as particles size are very small. In case of a true solution, no sediment settles down, showing that it is a stable medium. The beam of light passes through the transparent true solution without scattering.

**Suspensions** are translucent in thin sections while opaque in thick sections and its components can be separated by filtration. A residue is left behind on the filter paper after filtration. Also the beam of light neither passes through the suspension nor gets scattered.

**Colloids** are translucent solution and its components cannot be separated by filtration. In case of a colloidal solution, no sediment settles down, showing that it is a stable medium. In this case, the beam of light gets scattered.

## Procedure

1. Take three test tubes and label them as *A*, *B* and *C*.
2. Mark each test tubes in the lower half with a sign of cross (×).
3. Place these test tubes on a test tube stand such that the mark (×) is on the opposite side of the test tubes.
4. Fill test tube *A* with true solution of common salt [Refer experiment 1(a)], test tube *B* with suspension of chalk powder [Refer experiment 1(b)] and test tube *C* with colloidal solution of egg albumin in water [Refer experiment 1(c)] [as shown in Fig. 1].

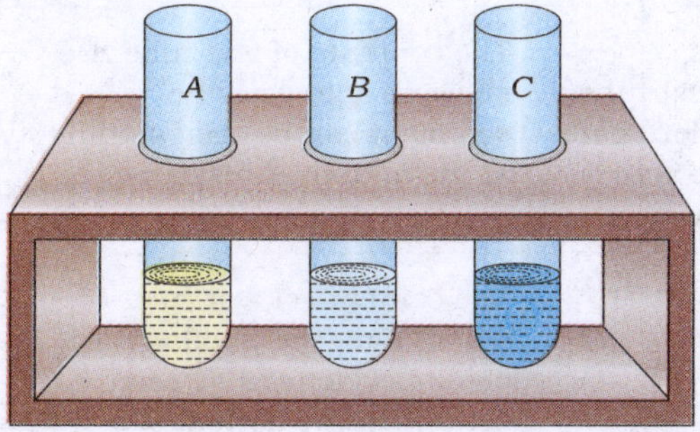


**Fig. 1** Test tubes containing a true solution, a suspension and a colloidal solution

## Observation

| S.N. | Property | Experiment | Observation | Inference |
|---|---|---|---|---|
| 1. | **Transparency** | Fill half of the test tube *A* with common salt solution. | The mark (×) is clearly visible when seen through the test tube *A*. | The common salt solution is transparent, and therefore, it is a true solution. |
| | | Fill half of the test tube *B* with the suspension of chalk powder. | The mark (×) is not visible when seen through the test tube *B*. | The suspension of chalk powder is opaque. So, it is a suspension. |
| | | Fill half of the test tube *C* with colloidal solution of egg albumin. [View through each sample and record your observations and inferences]. | The mark (×) is faintly visible when seen through the test tube *C*. | The solution of egg albumin is translucent. So, it is a colloidal solution. |
| 2. | **Filtration criterion** | Filter the contents of each test tube separately through a filter paper and collect the filtrate in three clean test tubes. Also label them as *D*, *E* and *F* respectively. Observe the filtrate and the residue left on the filter paper, if any as shown in Fig. 2. | In the case of test tube *A*, a clear filtrate is obtained (in test tube *D* ) and no residue is left on the filter paper. | Common salt cannot be separated from its solution in water by filtration. So, sample *A* is a true solution. |
| | | | In the case of test tube *B*, a clear filtrate is obtained (in test tube *E* ) and some residue (chalk powder) is left on the filter paper. | Chalk powder can be separated from its suspension in water by filtration. So, sample *B* is a suspension. |
| | | | In the case of test tube *C*, a translucent filtrate is obtained (in test tube *F*) and no residue is left on the filter paper. | Egg albumin cannot be separated from its colloidal solution in water by filtration. So, sample *C* is a colloidal solution. |
| 3. | **Stability** | Leave the test tubes (*A*, *B* and *C* ) on a test tube stand undisturbed for about 1-2 hours, and note your observations and inference. | The contents of test tube *A* show no change as no sediment can be seen settling at the bottom of test tube. | True solution of common salt in water is stable. |
| | | | The contents of test tube *B* show change as sediment of chalk powder can be seen settling at the bottom of test tube. The contents of test tube *C* show no change as no sediment can be seen settling at the bottom of test tube. | Suspension of chalk powder in water is unstable and the particles can be seen settling down under the influence of gravity. Colloidal solution of egg albumin in water is stable and particles do not settle down under the influence of gravity. |

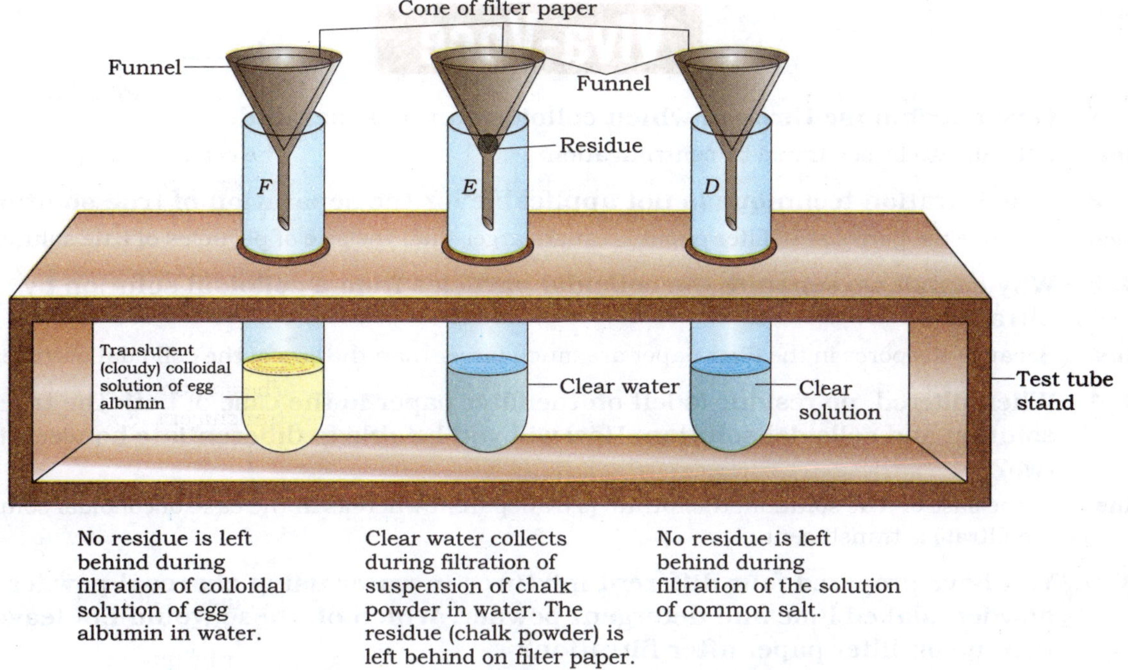


**Fig. 2** To distinguish between a true solution, a suspension and a colloidal solution on the basis of filtration

## Result

From the experiments performed, the following results are obtained

1. Common salt solution, i.e solution *A* is transparent, stable and its components cannot be separated by filtration.
2. The suspension of chalk powder in water, i.e solution *B* is opaque, unstable and its components can be separated by simple filtration.
3. The colloidal solution of egg albumin in water, i.e solution *C* is translucent, stable and its components cannot be separated by simple filtration.

### PRECAUTIONS

1. *Use a laboratory coat while carrying out the experiment.*
2. *Chalk should be grounded well in a mortar by using pestle to get a fine powder.*
3. *Use a separate glass rod for stirring the contents of the different test tubes.*
4. *All the solutions should be stirred well before observing.*
5. *Use proper lighting to observe transparency and Tyndall effect.*
6. *Label all the test tubes.*
7. *Handle the filtration setup carefully.*

## Suggested Experiments

1. Prepare a soap solution and sugar solution and study the properties of two solutions and write the observation in tabular form.
2. Prepare a solution of muddy water and a solution of ammonium chloride in water and observe their properties.

## Viva-Voce

**Q. 1 Give a technique through which colloids can be separated.**

**Ans.** Colloids can be separated by centrifugation.

**Q. 2 Why filtration technique is not applicable for the separation of true solution?**

**Ans.** Because the pore size of filter paper is much larger than the size of particles of true solutions.

**Q. 3 Why cannot we separate the colloidal particles from a colloidal solution by filtration?**

**Ans.** Because the pores in the filter paper are much larger than the size of the colloidal particles.

**Q. 4 When filtered, no residue is left on the filter paper in the case of both the true solution and colloidal solution. How will you be able to differentiate between the two?**

**Ans.** In the case of true solution, the filtrate is transparent whereas in the case of colloidal solution, the filtrate is translucent.

**Q. 5 You have prepared four different mixtures in water using charcoal powder, chalk powder, slaked lime and detergent powder. Which of these would not leave residue on filter paper after filtration?**

**Ans.** Detergent powder will not leave residue on filter paper after filtration as it is a colloidal solution. Charcoal powder, chalk powder and slaked lime in water are suspension and thus give residue on filter paper.

**Q. 6 The particles of which solution-true, colloidal and suspension, settle only by centrifugation?**

**Ans.** The particles of colloidal solution settle only by centrifugation.

**Q. 7 In an experiment to separate the components of a mixture of sand, common salt and ammonium chloride dissolved in water, the component of which substance will be removed by filtration?**

**Ans.** The component of sand will be removed by filtration. Common salt and ammonium chloride dissolve in water to form a true solution which cannot be removed by filtration.

## Questions From NCERT Lab Manual

**Q. 1 Classify the following as a true solution, suspension or colloids: milk, $CuSO_4$ solution, jam, gum, soil in water and sand in water**

**Ans.** True solution — $CuSO_4$ solution

Suspension — soil in water, sand in water

Colloids — milk, jam, gum

**Q. 2 What different techniques of separation can be employed for the separation of components of homogeneous and heterogeneous mixtures?**

**Ans.** Techniques that can be used to separate the components of homogeneous mixture are (i) evaporation (ii) distillation (iii) liquefication.

Techniques that can be used to separate the components of heterogeneous mixture are (i) filtration (ii) sedimentation and decantation (iii) separating funnel (iv) sublimation (v) chromatography.

## Practical Based MCQs

*For Experiments 1(a), 1(b), 1(c) and 1(d)*

**Q. 1 Which of the following is not a suspension?**

(a) Soil in water
(b) Sand in water
(c) Chalk powder in water
(d) Copper sulphate in water

**Q. 2 Tyndall effect is observed in**

(a) true solution
(b) starch + water
(c) alum + water
(d) table salt + water

**Q. 3 If common salt is added to the unsaturated solution of water and common salt, it will**

(a) become a colloid
(b) become a suspension
(c) start showing Tyndall effect
(d) remain a true solution

**Q. 4 In an experiment to separate the components of a mixture of sand, common salt and ammonium chloride dissolved in water, the component which will be removed by filtration is**

(a) sand
(b) common salt
(c) ammonium chloride
(d) None of these

**Q. 5 A suspension of chalk in water can be prepared**

(a) by placing a piece of chalk in water.
(b) by placing powdered chalk in water.
(c) by placing powdered chalk in water and shaking it vigorously.
(d) by placing powdered chalk in dil. HCl.

**Q. 6 Four students prepared mixtures in water by taking sodium chloride, sand, chalk powder and starch respectively, in four different test tubes. After stirring the mixture that appeared clear and transparent was that of**

(a) starch and water
(b) chalk powder and water
(c) sand and water
(d) sodium chloride and water

**Q. 7 A student mixes white part of an egg with water and stirs it well. After some time, he observes that**

(a) egg white settles at the bottom.
(b) egg white floats on the surface of water.
(c) a clear solution is formed.
(d) a cloudy solution is formed.

**Q. 8 The correct procedure for preparing a colloidal solution of egg albumin in water is**

(a) to break the egg shell, take only white portion and add it to water with constant stirring.
(b) to break the egg shell, take only the yellow portion and add it to boiling water with constant stirring.
(c) to boil the egg first, break the egg shell, add the white portion to the cold water and mix.
(d) to break the egg shell and take both white and yellow portions, further add it to boiling water with constant stirring.

**Q. 9 Which of the following pass through filter paper unchanged?**

(a) Soil and water
(b) Common salt and water
(c) Both (a) and (b)
(d) None of the above

**Q.10** **Following four unlabelled mixtures after stirring well were kept for observation and a student was asked to identify the transparent solution. His correct identification would be**

(a) copper sulphate + water (b) milk + water
(c) mud + water (d) starch + water

**Q.11** **Which of the following is most stable?**

(a) True solution (b) Colloidal solution
(c) Suspension (d) None of these

**Q.12** **A student was asked to prepare a true solution of sugar in water. By chance, he added sugar in excess. He stirred the solution for quite some time but some sugar settled down. He filtered the contents. The filtrate will be**

(a) true solution (b) colloidal solution
(c) suspension (d) true solution or colloidal solution

**Q.13** **Rohit mixed starch with water, boiled the mixture well and stirred it. He observed that**

(a) starch floats on the surface of water
(b) starch settles down at the bottom
(c) starch forms a translucent solution
(d) starch forms a transparent solution

**Q.14** **The colloidal solution where both the dispersed phase and the dispersion medium are liquids, is**

(a) milk
(b) shaving cream
(c) butter
(d) cheese

## Answers

| | | | | | | | |
|---|---|---|---|---|---|---|---|
| **1.** (d) | **2.** (b) | **3.** (d) | **4.** (a) | **5.** (c) | **6.** (d) | **7.** (d) | **8.** (a) |
| **9.** (b) | **10.** (a) | **11.** (a) | **12.** (d) | **13.** (c) | **14.** (a) | | |

# Experiment 2

## AIM

To prepare

(i) a mixture

(ii) a compound

Using iron filings and sulphur powder and distinguish between these on the basis of

(a) appearance, i.e. homogeneity and heterogeneity.

(b) behaviour towards a magnet.

(c) behaviour towards carbon disulphide as a solvent.

(d) effect of heat.

## Materials Required

China dish, pestle-mortar, petridish, watch glass, test tubes, glass rod, Bunsen burner, tripod stand, splinter (or candle), wire gauze, magnifying glass, bar magnet, funnel, filter paper, iron filings (10 g), sulphur powder (5 g), carbon disulphide (5 mL), dilute hydrochloric acid or dilute sulphuric acid, lead acetate solution.

## Theory/Principle

**Mixture** is a substance containing two or more elements or compounds in any proportion. The formation of mixture involves a physical change. Hence, its components retain their individual properties. These components can be separated by physical means. The appearance of a mixture can be homogeneous or heterogeneous. The mixture of iron filings (Fe) and sulphur powder (S) is heterogeneous in appearance. The components can be present in any proportion and their proportion can be changed. No energy change is involved in the preparation of a mixture.

Examples of mixture are air, sand, salt, iron filing and sulphur, etc. A mixture is not represented by any chemical formula and it does not have a fixed boiling point.

A **compound** is a pure substance which is formed by combination of two or more elements in definite proportion by mass. It is homogeneous in nature. The formation of a compound involves a chemical change. Hence, the components of a compound lose their individual properties and the resulting compound(s) acquire(s) new properties.

The components of a compound cannot be separated by physical means. Examples of compounds are common salt, water etc. A compound (e.g. iron sulphide, FeS ) is represented by a chemical formula and has a fixed melting and boiling points.

In a mixture of Fe (iron filings) and S (sulphur powder), the iron filings can be separated by means of a magnet and sulphur can be separated by dissolving in carbon disulphide ($CS_2$). However, iron sulphide (FeS) which is a compound, is neither attracted by the magnet nor it dissolves in carbon disulphide ($CS_2$).

## Procedure

1. **Preparation of mixture of iron** (Fe) **filing and sulphur**(S) **powder**

   Take 10g of iron filings and 5g sulphur powder in a pestle and mortar. Grind the constituents properly. The powder so obtained is a mixture of iron and sulphur. Keep it aside in a China dish and label this mixture as *A* as shown in Fig. 1(a).

2. **Preparation of a compound (FeS , iron sulphide) of iron filings and sulphur powder**

   Take one-half portion of the mixture in another China dish. Heat the mixture in the China dish slowly, stirring continuously with a glass rod, till a black mass is obtained as shown in Fig. 1(b). Then stop heating, and let the black mass cool.

$$\underset{\text{Iron}}{Fe(s)} + \underset{\text{Sulphur}}{S(s)} \xrightarrow{\text{Heat}} \underset{\text{Iron (II) sulphide}}{FeS(s)}$$

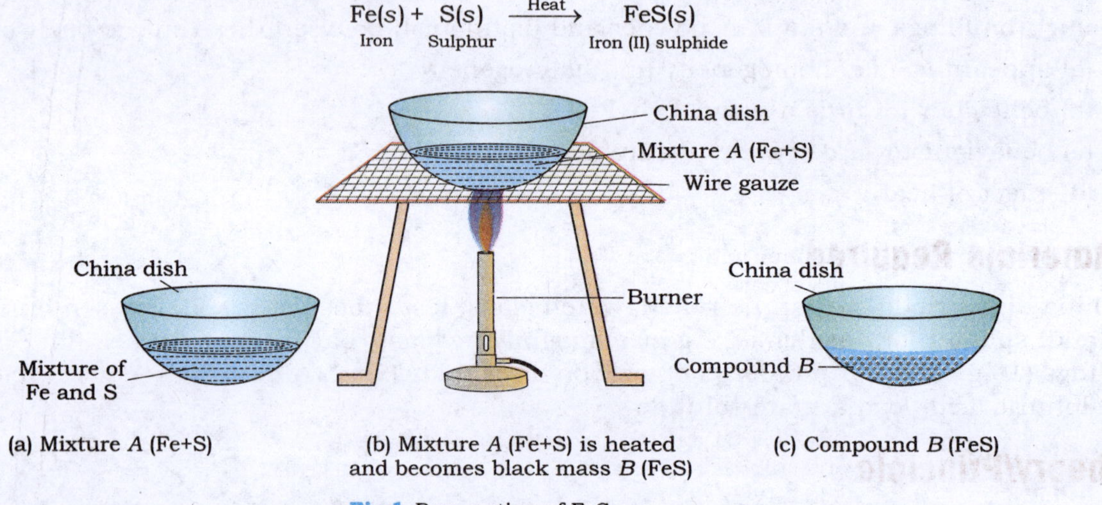


**Fig.1** Preparation of FeS

   Grind the solid black mass in a clean pestle and mortar to a fine powder. Keep it aside in a china dish. Label the powder of black mass as *B* as shown in Fig. 1(c).

3. **To distinguish between the compound and the mixture**

   Now take required amounts of mixture *A* and black mass *B* to conduct various tests as mentioned in the following table and record your observations and inferences in tabular form

## Observation Table

| S.N. | Test/Properties | Experiments | Observations | Inferences |
|---|---|---|---|---|
| 1. | **Appearance** | Take a small quantity of the mixture *A* prepared in a petridish. Observe it first with the naked eye and then with a magnifying glass. | Grey particles of iron and yellow particles of sulphur are seen clearly even with the naked eye. | The mixture *A* (Fe + S) is heterogeneous in appearance at room temperature. |
| | | Take a small quantity of the compound *B* of iron and sulphur in a petridish. Observe it first with the naked eye and then with a magnifying glass. | The whole mass appears uniform black in colour. | The compound *B* (FeS) is homogeneous in appearance. |

| | | | | |
|---|---|---|---|---|
| 2. | **Behaviour towards magnet** | Move a bar magnet over the prepared mixture *A* of iron and sulphur. 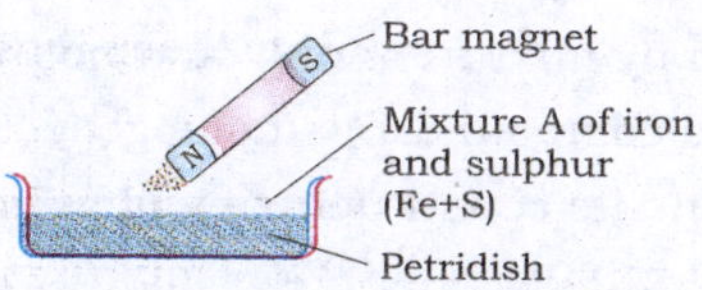<br>Bar magnet<br>Mixture A of iron and sulphur (Fe+S)<br>Petridish | Iron particles get attracted towards the magnet and sulphur is left behind. | The component elements of a mixture retain their properties. Iron retains its properties in mixture. |
| | | Move a bar magnet over the prepared compound *B* of iron and sulphur. 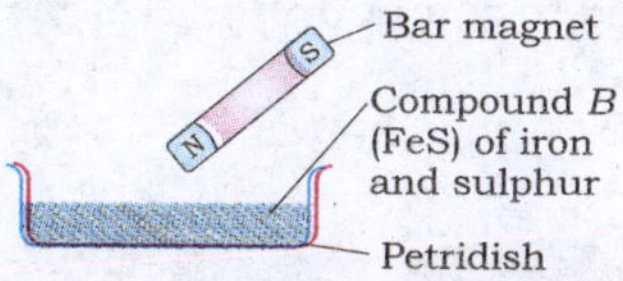<br>Bar magnet<br>Compound *B* (FeS) of iron and sulphur<br>Petridish | The black coloured particles of the compound *B* do not get attracted to the magnet. | The components forming a compound lost their properties. Iron has lost its properties of being attracted by magnet. |
| 3. | **Behaviour towards carbon disulphide ($CS_2$) as a solvent** | Take a small quantity of prepared mixture *A* of iron and sulphur in a test tube. Add 1-2 mL of carbon disulphide. Shake well and filter. Collect the filtrate in a China dish. Let carbon disulphide evaporate. | Carbon disulphide ($CS_2$) dissolves sulphur and iron particles are left on filter paper. Yellow sulphur crystals can be seen in the China dish after carbon disulphide has evaporated. | The components forming a mixture can be separated by simple physical methods. |
| | | Take a small quantity of the prepared compound *B* of iron and sulphur in a test tube. Add 1-2 mL of carbon disulphide to it and shake well. | The compound of iron and sulphur does not dissolve in carbon disulphide. | Constituents of a compound cannot be separated by simple physical methods. |
| 4. | **Effect of heat** | Take a small quantity of the prepared mixture *A* of iron and sulphur in a China dish and heat it. | At higher temperature, iron and sulphur react to form a black coloured substance which does not show the properties of iron and sulphur. | The components of the mixture *A* of iron and sulphur react on heating to give a compound *B* called iron sulphide.<br>$Fe\,(s) + S\,(s) \xrightarrow{\text{Heat}} \underset{\text{Iron sulphide}}{FeS(s)}$ |
| | | Take a small quantity of the prepared compound *B* of iron and sulphur in a China dish and heat it. | No reaction occurs. The substance on strong heating, starts glowing and on cooling, it returns to its original colour. | The compound *B* (iron sulphide) remains chemically unchanged on heating. |
| 5. | **Reaction with dilute sulphuric acid, $H_2SO_4$ (*aq*) or dilute hydrochloric acid, HCl (*aq*)** | Take a small quantity of the prepared mixture *A* of iron and sulphur in a boiling tube. Add 1-2 mL of dilute $H_2SO_4$ and heat it. Bring burning splinter or lighted candle near the mouth of the boiling tube. | Bubbles of a colourless and odourless gas are evolved which burns with a blue flame with a popping sound. Yellow powder (sulphur) remains unreacted. | Iron reacts with dilute $H_2SO_4$ to give hydrogen gas.<br>$2Fe(s) + 3H_2SO_4(aq) \longrightarrow Fe_2(SO_4)_3(aq) + 3H_2(g)$<br>$2Fe(s) + 6HCl\,(aq) \longrightarrow 2FeCl_3(aq) + 3H_2(g)$ |
| | | Take a small quantity of the prepared compound *B* of iron and sulphur in a test tube. Add 1-2 mL of dilute $H_2SO_4$ or dilute HCl. Bring a filter paper dipped in lead acetate solution near the mouth of the test tube. | A gas having the smell of rotten eggs is evolved which turns lead acetate paper into shiny black. | The liberated gas is hydrogen sulphide.<br>$FeS(s) + H_2SO_4(aq) \longrightarrow FeSO_4(aq) + H_2S(g)$<br>$FeS(s) + 2HCl\,(aq) \longrightarrow FeCl_2(aq) + H_2S(g)$<br>$(CH_3COO)_2\,Pb(aq) + H_2S(g) \longrightarrow \underset{\text{(Black)}}{PbS(s)} + 2CH_3COOH\,(aq)$ |

## Result

1. When iron filings and sulphur powder are mixed together, a mixture'*A*' (Fe + S) is obtained. When this mixture is heated, a compound '*B*' (FeS) is obtained.
2. Magnetic behaviour towards magnet is shown by mixture *A* only and not by compound *B*.
3. The mixture *A* is heterogeneous in nature and compound *B* is homogeneous in nature.
4. Constituents of mixture *A* can be separated into its constituents by physical methods (dissolving in $CS_2$) but constituents of compound *B* cannot be separated out.
5. On heating strongly, iron and sulphur (mixture) combine chemically to form FeS. However, heat has no effect on compound FeS.
6. When dil. $H_2SO_4$ is added to mixture *A*, a colourless and odourless $H_2$ gas is obtained which burns with pop sound whereas when dil. $H_2SO_4$ is added to compound *B*, $H_2S$ gas with a smell of rotten eggs is obtained.

### PRECAUTIONS

1. Do not heat the mixture of iron and sulphur in an ordinary glass tube, as the test tube may crack due to strong heating. Use a China dish or a boiling tube to heat the mixture.
2. Keep $CS_2$ away from the flame, as it is flammable.
3. Do not touch the pieces of the black mass (FeS) with bare hands to avoid injury, use forceps while observing FeS pieces in the experiment.
4. Do not inhale gases evolved directly.
5. Use a small amount of the mixture or compound for performing various experiments.

## Suggested Experiments

1. Explain the process used to separate a mixture of iron filings, ammonium chloride and common salt.
2. Prepare a homogeneous solution of copper sulphate in water and a heterogeneous mixture of iron filings and sulphur and compare their properties.

## Viva-Voce

**Q. 1 What happens when a mixture of iron and sulphur is heated with dil. $H_2SO_4$? What kind of change occur during this process?**

**Ans.** Sulphur present in the mixture, does not react with dil. $H_2SO_4$. Iron reacts with dil. $H_2SO_4$ and on heating, hydrogen gas is liberated. A chemical change occurs.

$$\underset{\text{From mixture}}{Fe(s)} + H_2SO_4(aq) \xrightarrow{\text{Heat}} \underset{\text{Iron sulphate}}{FeSO_4(aq)} + H_2 \uparrow$$

**Q. 2 A student by mistake mixed iron filings and sulphur powder. He wanted to separate them from each other. Which method should he use to separate the mixture?**

**Ans.** Dissolve mixture in carbon disulphide. Sulphur will dissolve while iron will not. On filtration, iron will be separated.

**Q. 3 Priya took small amount of mixture of iron and sulphur powder in a test tube and to it she added 15 mL of carbon disulphide. The test tube was vigorously shaken. What did she observed?**

**Ans.** She observed that the yellow coloured sulphur particles was dissolved in carbon disulphide ($CS_2$) but iron was not dissolved in $CS_2$.

**Q. 4** **Is air a mixture or chemical compound? Is it homogeneous or heterogeneous?**

**Ans.** Air is a mixture it commonly contains dust, smoke particles and other suspended impurities. So, air is a heterogeneous mixture. However, pure and clean air is a homogeneous mixture of gases.

**Q. 5** **Which is the most appropriate method for separating iron filings from sulphur present in a mixture?**

**Ans.** Using a bar magnet, iron filings can be separated from a mixture of iron and sulphur.

**Q. 6** **Iron from the mixture of iron and suphur is attracted by a magnet but not that in compound of iron sulphide. Give reason.**

**Ans.** In case of mixture, iron retains its identity but in case of compound, it is chemically combined. So, it is attracted in case of mixture but not in compound.

**Q. 7** **What change in colour is observed when a mixture of iron filings and sulphur is heated?**

**Ans.** The initial colour is yellow due to sulphur powder whereas on heating, iron sulphide is formed which is black in colour.

**Q. 8** **The properties of the product of an operation are different from those of the constituents'. State whether this product is an element, compound or a mixture.**

**Ans.** This product is a compound because the properties of product are different from those of the constituents in a compound.

**Q. 9** **Classify the following as a mixture/compound: Air, water, iron sulphide, brine solution, alloys.**

**Ans.** **Mixture** Air, brine solution, alloys.

**Compound** Iron sulphide, water.

**Q.10** **Which process is used to separate a mixture of iron filings, iodine and common salt?**

**Ans.** Magnet will remove iron filings, iodine will sublime (i.e. change directly into vapours and gets separated). Common salt will be left behind.

**Q.11** **Mohan heated a mixture of sulphur and iron filings in a China dish till a grey black product was formed. After that, he added 3 mL carbon disulphide to it and stirred the contents. What did he observe on stirring?**

**Ans.** He observed that no change takes place as there will be no reaction between carbon disulphide and iron sulphide.

## Question From NCERT Lab Manual

**Q. 1** **How would you proceed to test that a mixture of $NH_4Cl$ and $CuSO_4$ give test for $NH_4^+$, $Cl^-$, $Cu^{2+}$ and $SO_4^{2-}$ ions?**

**Ans.** **Test for $NH_4^+$** Bring a rod dipped in conc. HCl near the mouth of the test tube containing a mixture of $NH_4Cl$ and $CuSO_4$. White dense fumes are observed near the mouth of the test tube confirming the presence of $NH_4^+$ ions.

**Test for $Cl^-$** Add a few drops of silver nitrate ($AgNO_3$) solution into the test tube containing the mixture. A white precipitate is formed confirming the presence of $Cl^-$ ions.

**Test for $Cu^{2+}$** Add ammonium hydroxide solution in excess to the mixture. Deep blue colour confirms the presence of $Cu^{2+}$ ions.

**Test for $SO_4^{2-}$** Take 2 mL of sodium carbonate extract and add dil. HCl. Heat to let $CO_2$ gas escape. Cool and add 1 mL of $BaCl_2$ solution. White precipitate confirms the presence of $SO_4^{2-}$ ions.

## Practical Based MCQs

**Q. 1 In the experiment shown below, a gas is evolved. Four groups of students have recorded their observations on the gas produced as shown in the following table. The positive response are shown by '✓' and negative by '✗' signs, respectively.**

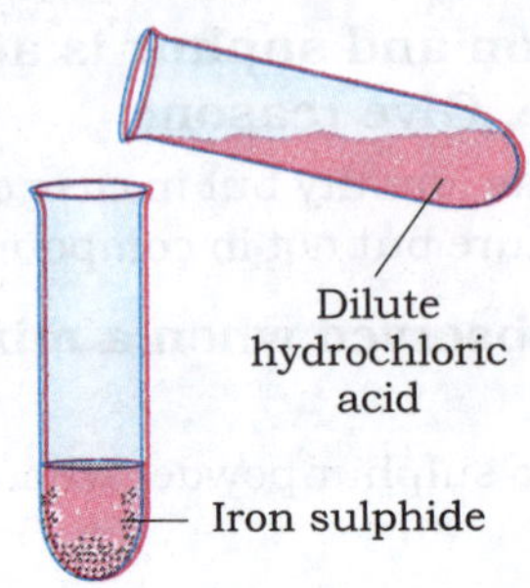


| | Colour of the gas | Odour of the gas | Flammability | Action on lead acetate paper |
|---|---|---|---|---|
| *A* | ✗ | ✓ | ✓ | ✗ |
| *B* | ✗ | ✓ | ✗ | ✓ |
| *C* | ✓ | ✓ | ✗ | ✓ |
| *D* | ✗ | ✗ | ✓ | ✗ |

**Identify the correct set of observations.**

(a) *A* (b) *B* (c) *C* (d) *D*

**Q. 2 In an experiment, carbon disulphide was added to a test tube containing a mixture of iron filings and sulphur powder as shown in the given diagrams.**

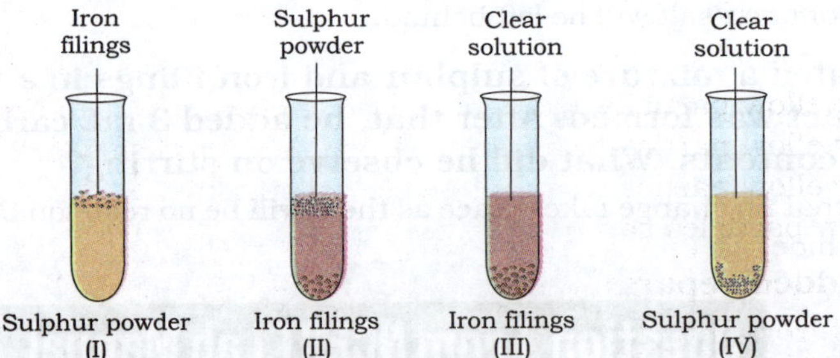


The correct observation is represented in diagram

(a) I (b) II (c) III (d) IV

**Q. 3 Four students took separately the sample of iron sulphide compound. A gas was liberated when each student added equal volume of dilute hydrochloric acid. They reported the following observations**

| Student | Colour of gas | Odour of gas | Flammability of gas |
|---|---|---|---|
| *A* | Colourless | Bad smell | Non-Inflammable |
| *B* | Colourless | Odourless | Non-Inflammable |
| *C* | Green | Bad smell | Inflammable |
| *D* | Yellow | No smell | Non-Inflammable |

The correct observations were reported by student

(a) *A* (b) *B* (c) *C* (d) *D*

**Q. 4** **Iron sulphide and a mixture of iron filings and sulphur powder were taken in different China dishes. Which of the following observations is correct?**

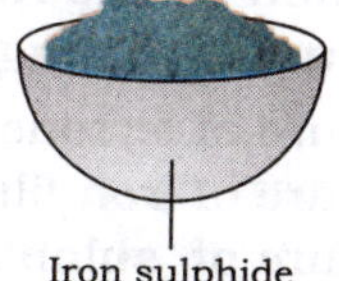
Iron sulphide

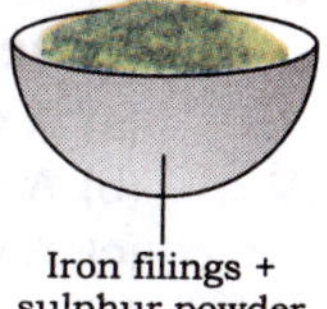
Iron filings + sulphur powder

(a) Both are heterogeneous.
(b) Both are homogeneous.
(c) Iron sulphide is homogeneous but the mixture of iron filings and sulphur is heterogeneous.
(d) Iron sulphide is heterogeneous while the mixture of iron filings and sulphur is homogeneous.

**Q. 5** **A student takes a substance *A*, which is attracted by a magnet and reacts with acids. He takes another substance *B*, which dissolves in carbon disulphide. He heats *A* and *B* together in a test tube to form product *AB*. The substance *A* and *B* and the product *AB* are respectively**

(a) *A*—Sulphur powder, *B*—Iron filings, *AB*—Iron sulphide
(b) *A*—Iron filings, *B*—Sulphur powder, *AB*—Iron sulphide
(c) *A*—Iron sulphide, *B*—Sulphur powder, *AB*—Iron filings
(d) *A*—Iron filings, *B*—Iron sulphide, *AB*—Sulphur powder

**Q. 6** **China dish *A* contains mixture of iron filings and sulphur powder. In China dish *B*, same portion of the mixture is heated till the two components combine together to form a compound. Umesh added carbon disulphide to both the China dishes. He would observe that**

(a) in China dish *A*, sulphur dissolves but in *B*, contents remain unaffected.
(b) in China dish *B*, sulphur component of the compound dissolves but in *A*, contents remain unaffected.
(c) sulphur dissolves in both the China dishes *A* and *B*.
(d) sulphur does not dissolve in either of the China dishes.

**Q. 7** **When you mix iron filings with sulphur powder thoroughly and spread the mixture evenly on a white sheet, how do the particles in the mixture appear?**

(a) Grey and yellow particles can be seen distinctly, spread uniformly.
(b) Grey and yellow particles can be seen distinctly, but they are not spread uniformly.
(c) Grey and yellow particles cannot be seen distinctly.
(d) Only yellow particles can be seen distinctly.

**Q. 8** **Dil.HCl is added separately to**

I. mixture of iron filings and sulphur.
II. iron sulphide.

**The correct observation is**

(a) iron sulphide reacts with HCl to give $H_2$ gas.
(b) mixture of iron filings and sulphur reacts with HCl to give $H_2S$ gas.
(c) iron sulphide does not react with HCl.
(d) mixture of iron filings and sulphur reacts with HCl to give $H_2$ gas.

**Q. 9** **Ferrous sulphide is formed**

(a) by heating iron filings with sulphuric acid.
(b) by heating iron filings with sulphur.
(c) by the reaction of mixture of iron filings and sulphur with dilute hydrochloric acid.
(d) by the reaction of iron with hydrogen sulphide gas.

**Q.10 From which of the following mixtures, the separation of the components may be done by using a magnet.**

(a) A mixture of ferrous sulphide and copper sulphide.
(b) A mixture of iron filings and ferrous sulphide.
(c) A mixture of sulphur powder and ferrous sulphide.
(d) A mixture of carbon disulphide and ferrous sulphide.

**Q.11 How do you separate a mixture of sulphur, iron filings and salt?**

(a) Use magnet, dissolve in water, filter and crystallise.
(b) Use magnet, filter, decant and crystallise.
(c) Dissolve in water, filter, crystallise and decant.
(d) Decant, crystallise, filter and dissolve in water.

**Q.12 When iron filings and sulphur powder are heated at high temperature in a China dish**

(a) no reaction takes place.
(b) yellow coloured compound is formed which is soluble in carbon disulphide.
(c) black coloured compound is formed which is insoluble in carbon disulphide.
(d) black coloured compound is formed which is attracted by magnet.

**Q.13 Which is not the property of a mixture?**

(a) Mixtures, are heterogeneous in nature.
(b) The composition of mixture always remain constant.
(c) The composition of mixture may show variability.
(d) Its elements/components are separated by physical methods.

**Q.14 In the laboratory, what precautions have to be taken with carbon disulphide?**

(a) Keep away from flame.
(b) Keep away from carbon.
(c) Keep away from distilled water.
(d) Keep away from iron sulphide.

## Answers

| | | | | | | |
|---|---|---|---|---|---|---|
| **1.** (b) | **2.** (c) | **3.** (a) | **4.** (c) | **5.** (b) | **6.** (a) | **7.** (b) |
| **8.** (d) | **9.** (b) | **10.** (b) | **11.** (a) | **12.** (c) | **13.** (b) | **14.** (a) |

# Experiment 3

## AIM

To perform the following reactions and classify them as physical or chemical changes:

(a) Iron with copper sulphate solution in water

(b) Burning of magnesium ribbon in air

(c) Zinc with dilute sulphuric acid

(d) Heating of copper sulphate crystals

(e) Sodium sulphate with barium chloride in the form of their solutions in water

## Materials Required

Iron nails, copper sulphate solution, test tubes, stand with clamp, sand paper, thread, test tube stand, magnesium ribbon, burner, tongs, watch glass, zinc granules, dilute sulphuric acid, conical flask, hydrated copper sulphate crystals, sodium sulphate solution and barium chloride solution.

## Theory/Principle

### Physical Change

A physical change is a process in which the chemical composition of the substance remains unchanged and does not result in the production of a new substance. A physical change involves a change only in the physical properties of the material. The reacting substance in a physical change can be recovered by simple physical methods. Hence, a physical change is reversible.

### Chemical Change

A chemical change is a process in which reacting substance gives rise to new substance(s) having different chemical composition and properties. The reacting substances in a chemical change cannot be recovered by simple physical methods. Hence, a chemical change is usually irreversible. A chemical change (chemical reaction) involves the breaking of bonds in the atoms of reacting substances and making of new bonds between the atoms of products. A chemical change is represented by a chemical reaction.

Different types of chemical reactions are as follows

(i) **Displacement reaction** The reaction in which a more reactive metal displaces a less reactive metal from its aqueous solution. e.g. Iron (Fe) with copper sulphate ($CuSO_4$) solution.

$$\underset{\text{(more reactive)}}{\underset{\text{Iron}}{Fe(s)}} + \underset{\text{(blue coloured)}}{\underset{\text{Copper sulphate}}{CuSO_4(aq)}} \longrightarrow \underset{\text{(light green)}}{\underset{\text{Ferrous sulphate}}{FeSO_4(aq)}} + \underset{\text{less reactive)}}{\underset{\text{Copper metal (displaced,}}{Cu(s)}}$$

(ii) **Combination reaction** When two or more substances combine to form a single product. e.g. Burning of magnesium in air

$$\underset{\text{Magnesium}}{2Mg(s)} + \underset{\text{(from air)}}{\underset{\text{Oxygen}}{O_2(g)}} \xrightarrow[\text{Burn with dazzling white light}]{\text{Heat}} \underset{\text{(white powder)}}{\underset{\text{Magnesium oxide}}{2MgO(s)}}$$

(iii) **Reaction of metals with acids** The reaction in which metals react with acid forming metal salt and liberate hydrogen gas. e.g. Zinc with dil. sulphuric acid.

$$\underset{\text{Zinc metal}}{Zn(s)} + \underset{\text{Sulphuric acid}}{H_2SO_4(aq)} \longrightarrow \underset{\text{Zinc sulphate}}{ZnSO_4(aq)} + \underset{\text{Hydrogen gas}}{H_2(g)}$$

It is also a type of displacement reaction.

(iv) **Decomposition reaction** The reaction in which a single substance breaks down into two or more simpler substances. e.g. Heating of copper sulphate.

$$\underset{\text{(Blue)}}{CuSO_4 \cdot 5H_2O(s)} \xrightarrow{\text{Heat}} \underset{\text{(White)}}{CuSO_4\ (s)} + 5H_2O$$

The above process is reversed, when water is added to anhydrous copper sulphate.

$$\underset{\text{(white)}}{CuSO_4(s)} + 5H_2O \longrightarrow CuSO_4 \cdot 5H_2O(s)$$

On further heating, anhydrous copper sulphate decomposes to form sulphur trioxide gas and copper oxide.

$$CuSO_4(s) \xrightarrow{\text{Heat}} CuO(s) + SO_3(g)$$

The whole change of heating of copper sulphate pentahydrate can be given by the following equation

$$\underset{\text{Copper sulphate pentahydrate}}{CuSO_4 \cdot 5H_2O(s)} \xrightarrow{\text{Heat}} \underset{\text{Copper oxide}}{CuO\ (s)} + \underset{\text{Sulphur trioxide}}{SO_3(g)} + \underset{\text{Water}}{5H_2O}$$

(v) **Double displacement reaction** The reactions in which there is an exchange of ions between the reactants. e.g. Sodium sulphate with barium chloride in the form of their solution in water.

$$\underset{\text{Sodium sulphate}}{Na_2SO_4(aq)} + \underset{\text{Barium chloride}}{BaCl_2(aq)} \longrightarrow \underset{\text{Barium sulphate}}{BaSO_4(s)} + \underset{\text{Sodium chloride}}{2NaCl\ (aq)}$$

## Procedure, Observation and Inference

### 1. Iron with Copper Sulphate Solution in Water

| S.N. | Experiments | Observations | Inferences |
|---|---|---|---|
| 1. | Take about 10 mL of $CuSO_4$ solution in a clean, dry test tube and drop a clean and rust free iron nail into it. Keep the test tube undisturbed for about 10 min [as shown in Fig. 1(a)]. | The blue coloured solution becomes light green in colour. | On reaction of iron nail with $CuSO_4$ solution, $FeSO_4$ is formed which is light green in colour and free Cu is formed which is deposited over the iron nail as a reddish brown deposit. This shows that iron is more reactive than copper as $Fe^{2+}$ ions have displaced $Cu^{2+}$ ions from copper sulphate solution. $\underset{\text{Copper sulphate}}{CuSO_4\ (aq)} + \underset{\text{Iron}}{Fe\ (s)} \longrightarrow \underset{\text{Ferrous sulphate}}{FeSO_4\ (aq)} + \underset{\text{Displaced copper}}{Cu\ (s)}$ It is a displacement reaction. |
| 2. | Remove the iron nails from the solution. Compare the intensity of blue colour of copper sulphate solution of both test tubes *A* and *B*. Also compare the colour of iron nail dipped in $CuSO_4$ solution which kept aside [as shown in Fig. 1(b)]. | The iron nail gets coated with a reddish brown deposit. | This is an example of **chemical change** as in this reaction, colour change, deposition of residue and the new substances are formed which have different properties. |

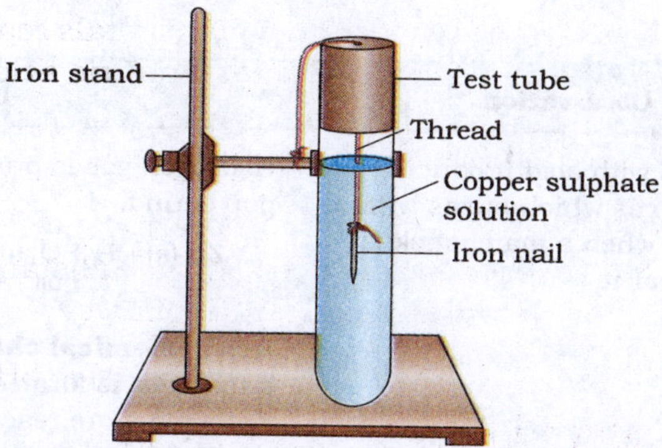


(a) Iron nails dipped in copper sulphate solution

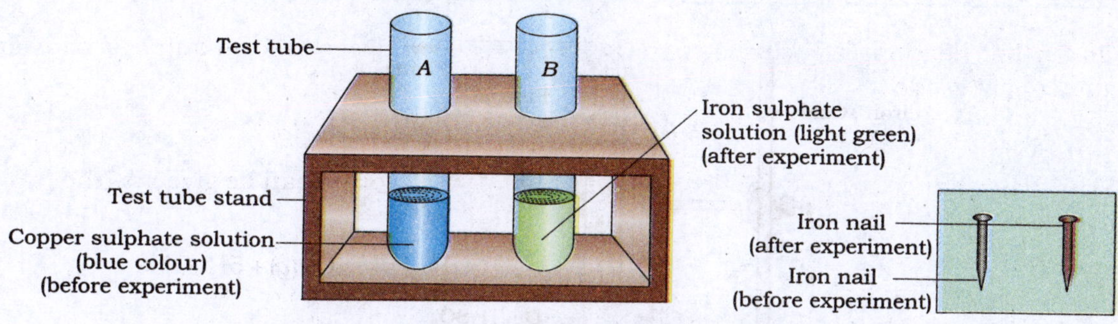


(b) Iron nails and copper sulphate solution compared before and after the experiment

**Fig. 1**

## 2. Burning of Magnesium in Air

| S.No. | Experiments | Observations | Inferences |
|---|---|---|---|
| 1. | Take a magnesium ribbon and rub it with sand paper to remove rust. Hold one end of about 5 cm of magnesium ribbon with a pair of tongs and bring a burning burner near the other end of the ribbon (as shown in Fig. 2). | The magnesium ribbon burns with a dazzling white flame to form a white powder which keeps dropping till the ribbon is burning. | Mg burns with $O_2$ to form a new chemical compound, MgO. $\underset{\text{Magnesium}}{2\,Mg\,(s)} + \underset{\text{Oxygen}}{O_2\,(g)} \longrightarrow \underset{\text{Magnesium oxide (white)}}{2MgO\,(s)}$ It is a combination reaction |
| 2. | Collect the white powder on a watch glass and add few drops of water. Dip a pH paper or red litmus strip in the solution. | The pH paper/red litmus strip turns blue. | MgO is basic in nature. Since, new substance is formed, so it is a **chemical change.** |

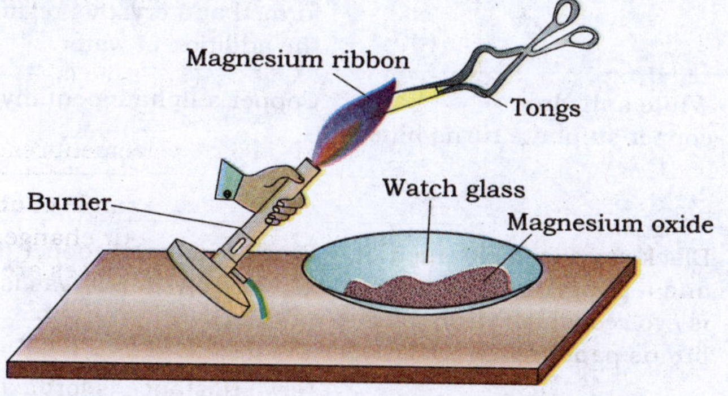


**Fig. 2** Burning of magnesium ribbon in air

## 3. Zinc with Dilute Sulphuric Acid

| Experiment | Observation | Inference |
|---|---|---|
| Take 2-3 pieces of granulated zinc in a test tube and to this, add about 5 mL of dilute sulphuric acid and observe (as shown in Fig. 3). | Zinc reacts with acid producing bubbles of gas which burns with a pop sound when a matchstick is brought near it. | Hydrogen gas is produced which burns with a pop sound. $Zn\,(s) + \underset{\text{Dil.}}{H_2SO_4(aq)} \longrightarrow ZnSO_4(aq) + H_2\uparrow$ It is a **chemical change** because a new substance is formed with the evolution of gas. Zn being more reactive displaces hydrogen from dil. $H_2SO_4$. Thus, it is a **displacement reaction.** |

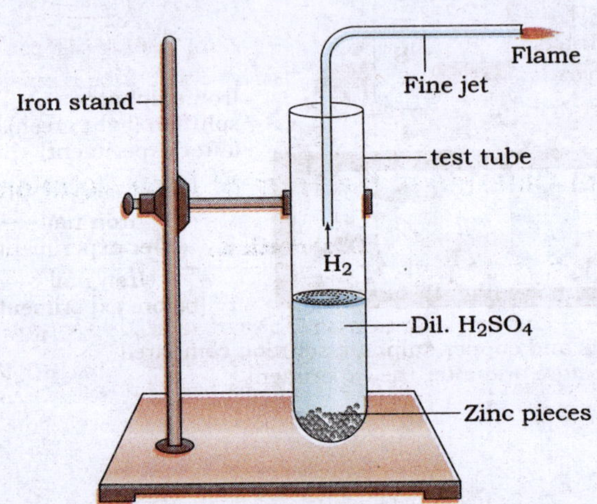


Fig. 3 Granulated zinc with dilute sulphuric acid

## 4. Heating of Copper Sulphate Crystals

| S.N. | Experiments | Observations | Inferences |
|---|---|---|---|
| 1. | Take small amount of hydrated copper sulphate crystals in a hard boiling tube and heat it over a flame [as shown in Fig. 4(a)]. | The crystals turn white due to loss of 5 molecules of water of crystallisation. | It forms anhydrous copper sulphate. Thus, it is a decompostion reaction and also called **dehydration reaction.** $\underset{\text{Copper sulphate pentahydrate}}{CuSO_4 \cdot 5H_2O\,(s)} \xrightarrow[\sim 150°C]{\Delta} \underset{\text{Anhydrous copper sulphate}}{CuSO_4}\,(s) + 5\,H_2O(l)$ This is a **physical change** as no new substance is formed and crystals regain their original colour on the addition of water. |
| 2. | Take anhydrous copper sulphate in another boiling tube and add a few drops of water. | White anhydrous copper sulphate turns blue. | Copper sulphate pentahydrate is regained. |
| 3. | Heat anhydrous copper sulphate strongly in the boiling tube and bring a moist blue litmus paper near the mouth of the boiling tube [as shown in Fig. 4(b)]. | Black residue is obtained and a pungent smelling gas is evolved which turns blue litmus paper red. | Black residue of copper oxide is formed and $SO_3$ gas is evolved. $SO_3$ gas is acidic in nature. $CuSO_4(s) \xrightarrow{250°C} CuO\,(s) + SO_3(g)\uparrow$ New substance is formed, so it is a **chemical change.** |

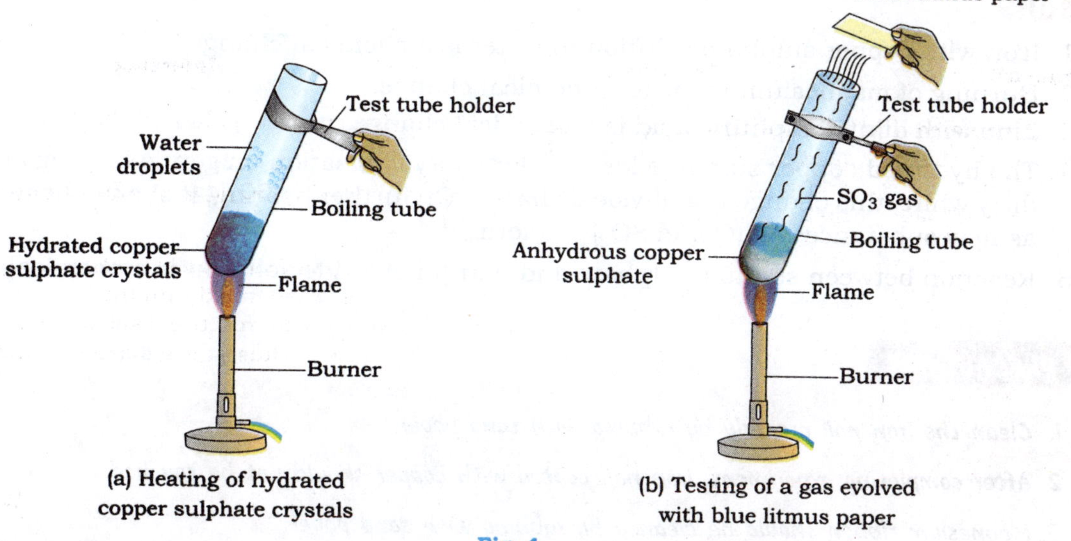


(a) Heating of hydrated copper sulphate crystals

(b) Testing of a gas evolved with blue litmus paper

**Fig. 4.**

## 5. Sodium Sulphate with Barium Chloride in the Form of Their Solutions in Water

| Experiment | Observation | Inference |
|---|---|---|
| Take a clean test tube *A* and put about 5 mL of $Na_2SO_4$ in it. Take another test tube *B* and put about 5 mL of $BaCl_2$ solution in it. Mix solution *B* in solution *A* carefully (as shown in Fig. 5). Keep the test tube undisturbed for sometime. | A white precipitate is formed which gradually settles at the base of the test tube. | $Na_2SO_4$ reacts with $BaCl_2$ solution to form insoluble $BaSO_4$.<br>$\underset{\text{Sodium sulphate}}{Na_2SO_4(aq)} + \underset{\text{Barium chloride}}{BaCl_2(aq)} \longrightarrow \underset{\text{Barium sulphate (white ppt).}}{BaSO_4\ (s)} + \underset{\text{Sodium chloride}}{2NaCl\ (aq)}$<br>It is a double displacement reaction<br>As new substances are formed, so it is a **chemical change.** |

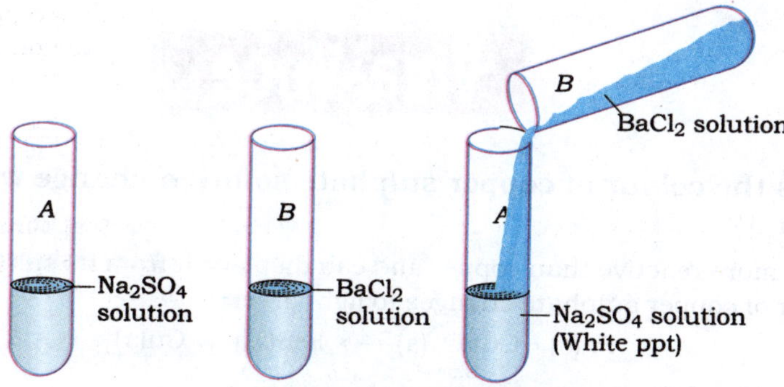


**Fig. 5** Preparation of $BaSO_4$ solution

## Results

1. Iron with copper sulphate solution in water is a chemical change.
2. Burning of magnesium in air is a chemical change.
3. Zinc with dilute sulphuric acid is a chemical change.
4. The hydrated copper sulphate loses water of crystallisation on gentle heating and become dirty white, this change is a physical change. On further heating, it shows chemical change as new substances ($CuO$ and $SO_3$) are formed.
5. Reaction between sodium sulphate and barium chloride solution is a chemical change.

### PRECAUTIONS

1. *Clean the iron nail properly by rubbing with sand paper.*
2. *After completing experiment, iron nail coated with copper should not be touched.*
3. *Magnesium ribbon should be cleaned by rubbing with sand paper.*
4. *Hold magnesium ribbon using tongs while burning it.*
5. *Since, magnesium ribbon burns with a dazzling bright flame, students should wear dark glasses.*
6. *Zinc granules should be cleaned before conducting the experiment.*
7. *Handle sulphuric acid with care.*
8. *Copper sulphate has a poisonous nature. So, it should be handled with care.*
9. *As sulphur trioxide is acidic in nature, its fumes should not be inhaled.*
10. *Do not disturb the mixture of barium chloride and sodium sulphate for 5-10 minutes, to allow the precipitate to form and settle down.*

## Suggested Experiments

1. To carry out the reaction between silver nitrate ($AgNO_3$) and sodium chloride ($NaCl$) and classify them as physical or chemical changes.
2. Study the effect of heat on lead nitrate crystals and classify them as physical or chemical change.

## Viva-Voce

**Q. 1 Why does the colour of copper sulphate solution change when an iron nail is dipped in it?**

**Ans.** Iron (Fe) is more reactive than copper and can displace it from its salt solution due to which the blue colour of copper sulphate changes to light green.

$$Fe(s) + \underset{\text{Blue}}{CuSO_4(s)} \longrightarrow \underset{\text{Green}}{FeSO_4(s)} + Cu(s)$$

**Q. 2 Why does the following reaction take place?**

$$2I^-(aq) + Cl_2(aq) \xrightarrow{CCl_4} 2Cl^-(aq) + I_2(\text{solvated})$$

**Ans.** The above reaction occurs because chlorine is more reactive than iodine and therefore, displaces iodide ions from solution.

**Q. 3 How does the combustion of hydrogen gas produce water?**

**Ans.**

$$\underset{\text{Hydrogen}}{2H_2(g)} + \underset{\text{Oxygen}}{O_2(g)} \longrightarrow \underset{\text{Steam}}{2H_2O(g)} + \text{Heat}$$

**Q. 4 Why should magnesium ribbon be cleaned before burning it in air?**

**Ans.** Magnesium ribbon should be cleaned before burning it in air to remove the oxide layer formed on it which makes it passive, so that it can ignite easily.

**Q. 5 How will you show that the hydrogen gas is neutral in behaviour?**

**Ans.** Hydrogen gas is neutral in behaviour because it neither turns red litmus paper blue nor it turns blue litmus paper red.

**Q. 6 Why does the red litmus paper turn blue when touched with aqueous solution of magnesium oxide?**

**Ans.** Aqueous solution of magnesium oxide is basic in nature because when magnesium oxide (MgO) is dissolved in water, it forms magnesium hydroxide $Mg(OH)_2$.

$$MgO(s) + H_2O \longrightarrow Mg(OH)_2(s)$$

So, aqueous solution of MgO turns red litmus paper blue.

**Q. 7 Is there a possibility of a compound other than MgO formed in the reaction of magnesium with air?**

**Ans.** Yes, magnesium also reacts with $N_2$ present in air to form magnesium nitride ($Mg_3N_2$).

$$3Mg(s) + N_2(g) \longrightarrow Mg_3N_2(s)$$

**Q. 8 Why is it suggested to wear dark coloured goggles while watching the burning of magnesium ribbon in air?**

**Ans.** It is suggested to wear dark coloured goggles to protect the eyes from intense white dazzling flame.

**Q. 9 Fill in the blanks.**

The white precipitate of barium sulphate is formed ......... (immediately/after some time) on mixing the solutions of sodium sulphate and barium chloride.

**Ans.** immediately

**Q.10 Which reaction takes place when magnesium burns in air? Why is it so called?**

**Ans.** Magnesium burns in air to give magnesium oxide and it is a combination reaction.

$$2Mg(s) + O_2(g) \xrightarrow{\Delta} 2MgO(s)$$

In this reaction, two reactants (Mg and $O_2$) combine to form a single product, magnesium oxide (MgO). Hence, it is called combination reaction.

**Q.11 What would you observe when dilute sulphuric acid is added to zinc granules in a test tube?**

**Ans.** When dilute sulphuric acid is added to zinc granules then bubbles start coming from the surface of the zinc granules.

**Q.12 Write the chemical reaction of zinc with dil. sulphuric acid.**

**Ans.**

$$\underset{\text{Zinc}}{Zn(s)} + \underset{\text{Sulphuric acid}}{H_2SO_4(aq)} \longrightarrow \underset{\text{Zinc sulphate}}{ZnSO_4(aq)} + \underset{\text{Hydrogen}}{H_2(g)}$$

**Q.13 A student took about 10 mL of dil. $H_2SO_4$ in a conical flask and added a few pieces of clean zinc metal. He observed small bubbles of a colourless and odourless gas coming out of the flask. On bringing a candle flame at the mouth of the flask, he observed that the candle flame goes off and the gas in the flask burns with a pop sound. Name the gas evolved.**

**Ans.** Hydrogen gas ($H_2$) is evolved.

**Q.14** **When copper sulphate crystals are heated in a test tube, what happens to the colour of the crystals?**

**Ans.** The colour of the crystal changes to white.

**Q.15** **When copper sulphate pentahydrate is heated to 650° C, then what is the nature of the condensed vapour?**

**Ans.** At 650°C, anhydrous copper (II) sulphate decomposes to form copper (II) oxide and sulphur trioxide gas which is acidic in nature.

**Q.16** **What kind of change is observed when an aqueous solution of sodium sulphate and barium chloride is mixed together?**

**Ans.** It is a chemical change where exchange of ions takes place.

## Practical Based MCQs

**Q. 1** **The gas evolved when zinc reacts with dilute sulphuric acid is**

(a) colourless, odourless and burns with a pop sound.
(b) colourless, foul smelling and burns with a pop sound.
(c) colourless, pungent smelling and burns with a pop sound.
(d) brown coloured, pungent smelling and does not burn.

**Q. 2** **An iron nail is placed in a beaker containing copper sulphate solution. In the beaker, a sensitive thermometer is suspended and the temperature of copper sulphate solution is recorded. The nail is taken out after 10 min and the temperature is again recorded. The thermometer at the end of experiment records**

(a) higher temperature
(b) lower temperature
(c) no change in temperature
(d) change in temperature depends upon the amount of copper sulphate solution taken

**Q. 3** **When solution of sodium sulphate is added to the solution of barium chloride, we immediately get a precipitate. Which of the following diagrams make correct identification of the precipitate?**

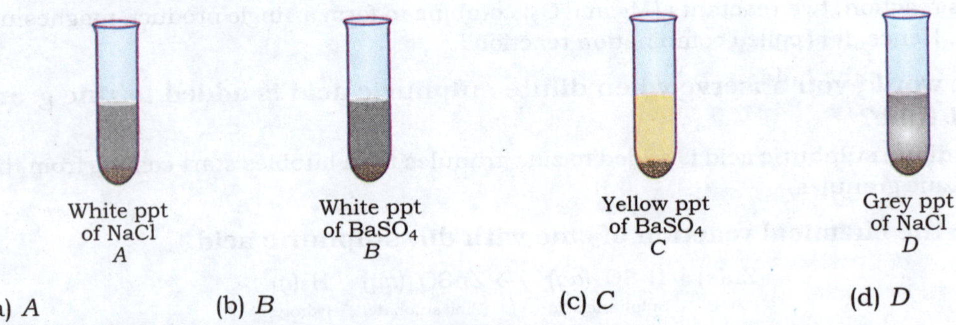


(a) *A* (b) *B* (c) *C* (d) *D*

**Q. 4** **Heating of crystals of copper sulphate leads to**

(a) change in colour
(b) cracking sound
(c) water droplets along the sides of test tube
(d) All of the above

**Q. 5** **Four students used different ways of burning magnesium ribbon during an experiment as shown below.**

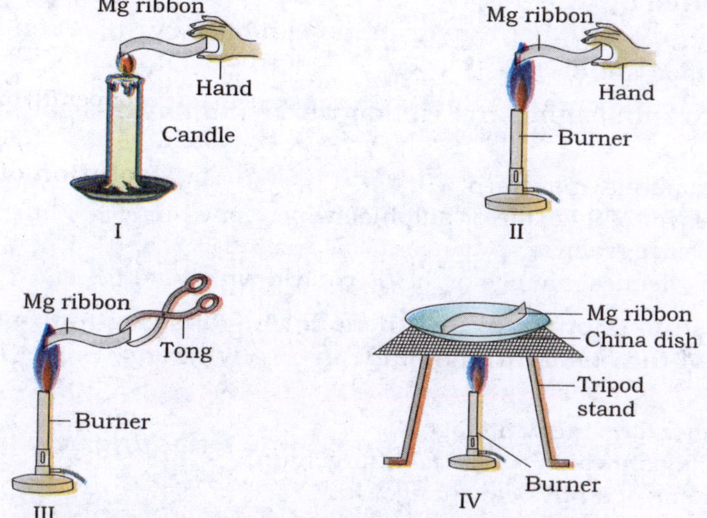


The correct way has been followed by the student

(a) I (b) II (c) III (d) IV

**Q. 6** **What is the correct description of $X, Y$ and $Z$ in the following figure with the heating of substance?**

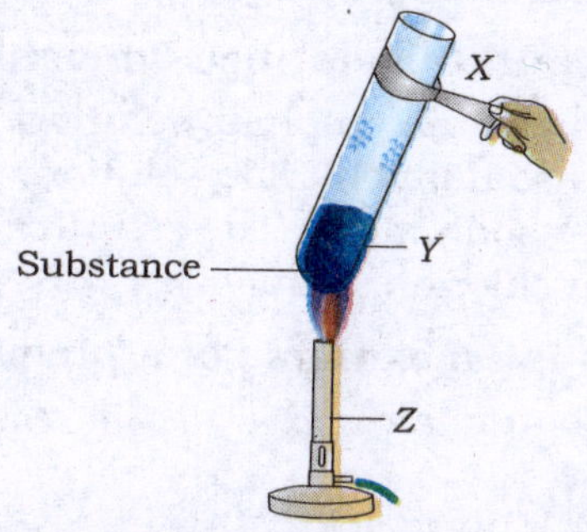


(a) $X$ = Test tube, $Y$ = Burner, $Z$ = Test tube holder
(b) $X$ = Test tube holder, $Y$ = Burner, $Z$ = Test tube
(c) $X$ = Test tube holder, $Y$ = Test tube, $Z$ = Burner
(d) $X$ = Test tube, $Y$ = Test tube holder, $Z$ = Burner

**Q. 7** **You are asked to study the reaction between zinc and dilute sulphuric acid. The apparatus required will be**

(a) test tubes, conical flask, burner and splinter
(b) test tube, test tube holder, burner and splinter
(c) test tubes, iron stand, matchbox and fine jet
(d) conical flask, delivery tube, rubber stopper, and matchbox

**Q. 8** **Some of the possible changes that may occur on strongly heating of crystals of copper sulphate are classified as**

**I. Physical change** **II. Chemical change**

**III. Reversible change** **IV. Irreversible change**

Which one of the above changes actually take place?

(a) Only I (b) I and III (c) I and IV (d) II and IV

**Q. 9** **Student $X$ puts Fe nails in $CuSO_4$ solution while the other student $Y$ puts Cu pieces in $FeSO_4$ solution. The observation that solution turns green from blue colour is reported by**

(a) Student $X$
(b) Student $Y$
(c) Both students $X$ and $Y$
(d) None of these

**Q.10** **It is advised to rub magnesium ribbon with sand paper before burning it in air because it**

(a) is very hard and may not burn.
(b) may have a layer of its oxide or sulphide which may hinder its burning.
(c) will become more reactive.
(d) undergoes a chemical change on being rubbed with sand paper.

**Q.11** **When magnesium is burnt in air, the following observations were recorded by Asmita. One of the observations made is totally wrong. Select the one which is wrong.**

(a) It burns with a dazzling white light.
(b) It forms white ash which turns red litmus blue.
(c) It is an example of a physical change.
(d) The ash formed is very light.

**Q.12** **Rubbing of magnesium ribbon with sand paper or any other abrasive will**

(a) alter its physical properties.
(b) alter its chemical properties.
(c) result in a chemical change.
(d) have no affect on its physical or chemical properties.

**Q.13** **Neeta observed that a precipitate is formed when she adds**

(a) barium chloride solution to sodium sulphate solution.
(b) barium chloride solution to sodium chloride solution.
(c) sodium sulphate solution to sodium chloride solution.
(d) hydrochloric acid to barium chloride solution.

**Q.14** **Which one of the following is an example of a physical change?**

(a) Burning of magnesium ribbon in air
(b) Burning of a candle
(c) Mixing of zinc and dilute sulphuric acid
(d) Boiling of water

**Q.15** **Iron filings were added to a solution of copper sulphate. After 10 min, it was observed that the blue colour of the solution changes and a layer gets deposited on iron filings. The colour of the solution formed and that of coating on iron filings would be**

(a) yellow and green
(b) brown and blue
(c) red and greenish-blue
(d) green and reddish-brown

## Answers

| | | | | | |
|---|---|---|---|---|---|
| **1.** (a) | **2.** (a) | **3.** (b) | **4.** (d) | **5.** (c) | **6.** (c) |
| **7.** (d) | **8.** (d) | **9.** (a) | **10.** (b) | **11.** (c) | **12.** (d) |
| **13.** (a) | **14.** (d) | **15.** (d) | | | |

# Experiment 4(a)

## AIM

To prepare stained, temporary mount of onion peel and to record observation and draw labelled diagram.

## Materials Required

An onion bulb, needles, brush, forceps, watch glasses, slides, petri dish, cover slips, blade, blotting paper, methylene blue/safranin solution, dropper, glycerine, water and a compound microscope.

## Theory/Principle

All living organisms are composed of cells. A cell is the structural and functional unit of life and new cells arises by the division in pre-existing cells. A typical plant cell consists of following basic structures (as shown in Fig. 1):

(a) **Cell wall** Outermost rigid covering of the plant cell.

(b) **Cell/Plasma membrane** The membrane beneath the cell wall enclosing cytoplasm, cell organelles and a nucleus. It is selectively permeable, allowing certain substances to enter and exit the cell.

(c) **Cytoplasm** A jelly-like substance present inside the cell, between the nucleus and cell membrane. It contains many specialised cell organelles.

(d) **Cellular organelles** These include endoplasmic reticulum, vacuoles, nucleus, plastids (only in plant cells), mitochondria, Golgi bodies, ribosomes, etc.

Animal and plant cells are different from each other as plant cells have cell wall and green coloured chloroplasts (a type of plastid, which is the site for photosynthesis) and animal cells have centrioles.

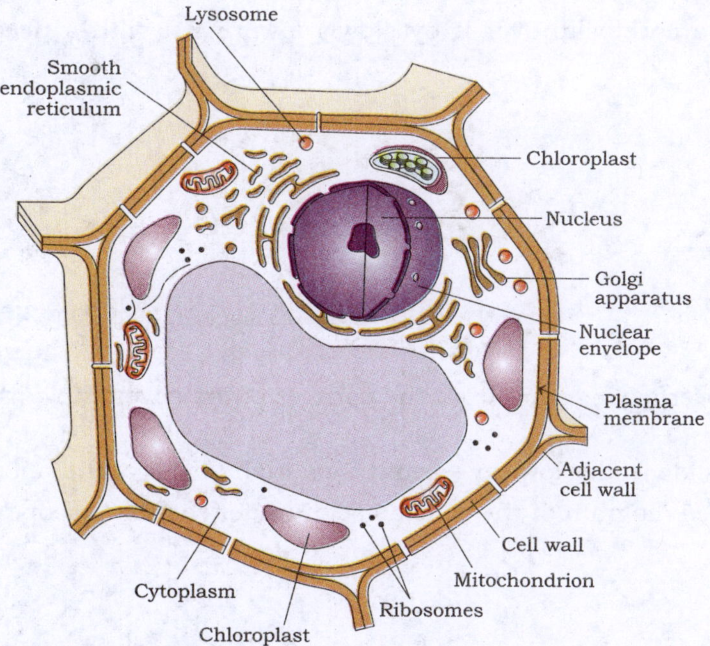


**Fig. 1** A typical plant cell and its various components

## Procedure (Preparation of Onion peel cell mount)

1. Take a piece of onion and remove one fresh leaf scale from it.

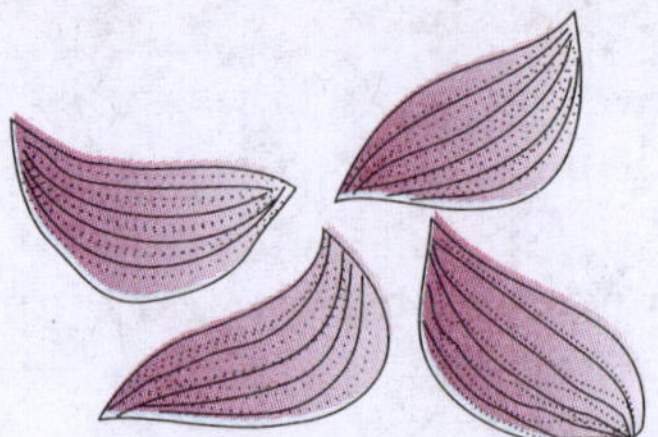

Fig. 2(a) Piece of onion bulb

2. Hold the scale and break it into two. Using a forcep, pull out the thin membranous peel, i.e. epidermal peel, adhering to the inner surface of this leaf scale.

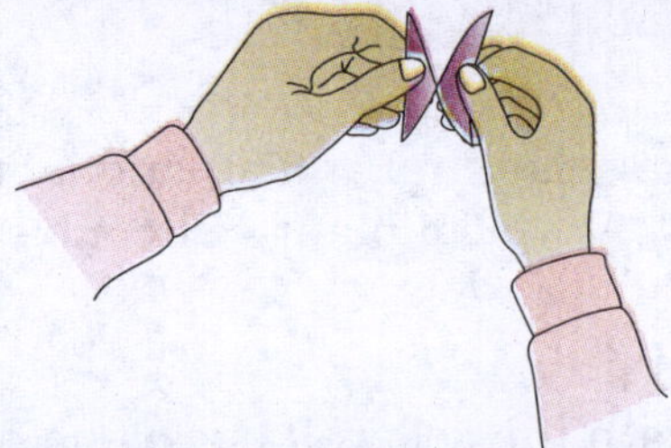

Fig. 2(b) Snap the scale backwards

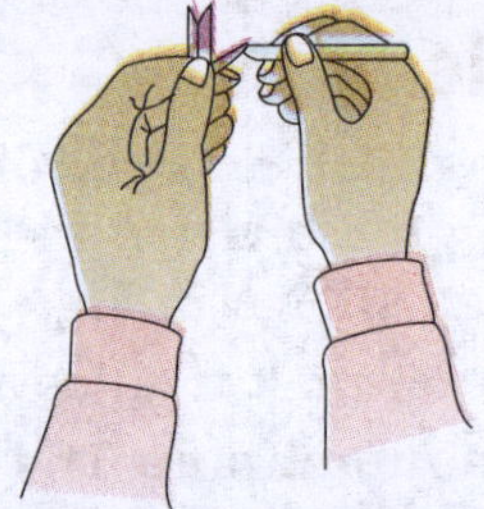

Fig. 2(c) Pull the transparent peel

3. Keep this peel in watch glass having some water to avoid dehydration of the onion peel cells.
4. Put 1-2 drops of safranin solution or methylene blue stain with a dropper in a petri dish having the onion peel and leave it there for 2-3 minutes to take up the stain.
5. Take water in another watch glass and dip the peel into it to remove excess stain.
6. After washing this peel with water, transfer it, by using a brush, onto the centre of a clean slide.
7. Now put a drop of glycerine on the peel to avoid drying up.
8. Gently place a cover slip over it by slowly lowering it with a needle. Avoid entry of air bubbles.

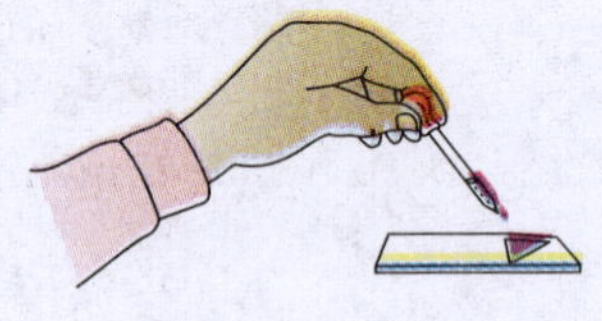

Fig. 2(d) Put the peel onto the slide

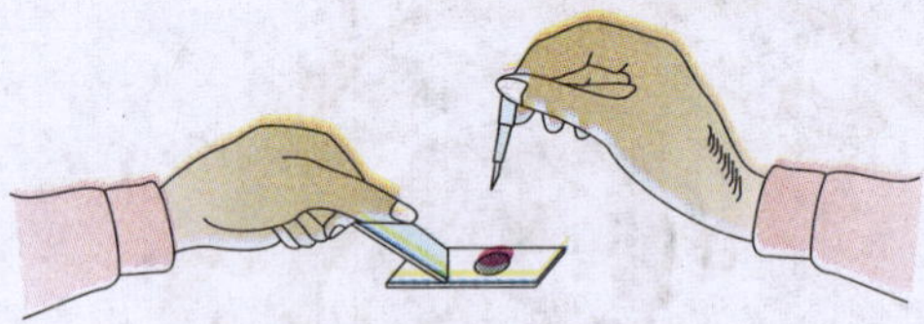

Fig. 2(e) Put drop of safranin first and then glycerine

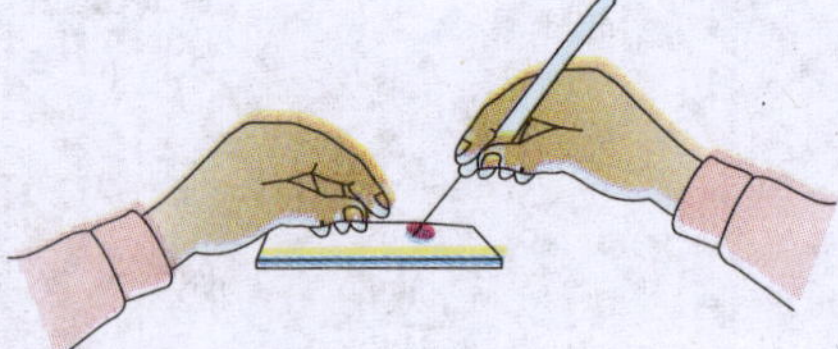

Fig. 2(f) Cover it with a cover slip.

9. Remove the overflowing fluid from the corners of the cover slip with the help of a blotting paper.
10. Observe the slide under low power and then high power of the microscope.
11. Draw a labelled diagram of the cells as seen under the microscope and note the features.

## Observations

Under different objectives (powers) of the compound microscope, onion peel cells can be visualised as shown in Fig. 3.

1. The cells of the onion peel are rectangular in shape.
2. Cells are arranged without any intercellular spaces. Just like a brick wall, lying side-by-side in a membrane.
3. Each cell has a distinct cell wall, a nucleus and a vacuole.

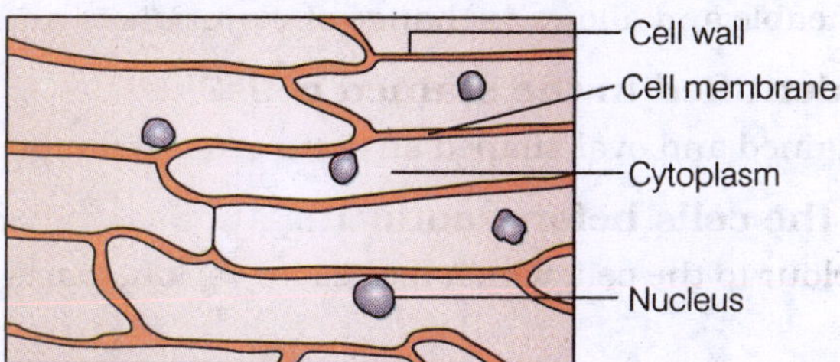


**Fig. 3** Epidermal cells of onion peel as observed under microscope

### PRECAUTIONS

1. *Staining of peel is an important process, make sure the peel is stained satisfactorily.*
2. *Excess stain should be removed by rinsing the peel in water, taken in a watch glass.*
3. *Placement of cover slip should be such that no air bubbles are formed.*
4. *A clean brush should be used to transfer the peel onto the slide.*
5. *Mount the peel on the centre of the slide.*
6. *Do not touch or force the cover slip directly by hand.*
7. *Always hold the slide from its edges.*
8. *Extra glycerine from the edges of the cover slip should be soaked with blotting paper.*

## Suggested Experiment

Prepare temporary mounts of cells from different plant sources like leaf peel, onion root tip, etc. Now study the cell's shape, size and their internal structures.

**Note** We will find that the cells from different sources are of different shapes and sizes besides having certain specific structures.

# Viva-Voce

**Q. 1 To prepare and observe the cells of an onion peel, what types of leaf/scale should be used?**

**Ans.** Thin membrane from a fleshy scale of onion must be used.

**Q. 2 The freshly removed onion peel is**

**(a) very delicate and membranous** **(b) red, hard and stiff**

**(c) very thick, hard** **(d) paperlike, coloured**

**Ans.** (a) very delicate and membranous

**Q. 3** **A necessary precaution while preparing a slide is to avoid air bubble formation. Why?**

**Ans.** Air bubbles interferes with the observation and make it difficult to recognise different cell organelles.

**Q. 4** **Name the plastid responsible for photosynthesis in plant cell.**

**Ans.** Chloroplast

**Q. 5** **State the importance of having a cell membrane in a cell.**

**Ans.** Cell membrane acts as a boundary and encloses cytoplasm, cell organelles and a nucleus. It is also selectively permeable and allows exchange of materials to and from the cell.

**Q. 6** **How is nucleus identified in the stained cells?**

**Ans.** Nucleus is a dark-stained and oval shaped structure found almost in the centre of the cell.

**Q. 7** **Why do we stain the cells before mounting?**

**Ans.** Staining provides colour to the cell, which makes its various parts to be more visible under microscope.

**Q. 8** **Glycerine is added after staining of the peel. Why can't we add it before staining?**

**Ans.** Glycerine forms a protective layer on the surface hence, the peel would not be able to absorb the stain. Therefore, it is added after staining to avoid drying up of the cells.

## Questions From NCERT Lab Manual

**Q. 1** **What is the size of nucleus in relation to size of cell?**

**Ans.** Nucleus is a samll part of the complete cell.

**Q. 2** **Name the stained parts of the cell.**

**Ans.** Stained parts of the cell are its nucleus, cytoplasm, cell wall and cell membrane.

**Q. 3** **Which of the following is a correctly labelled cell of an onion peel?**

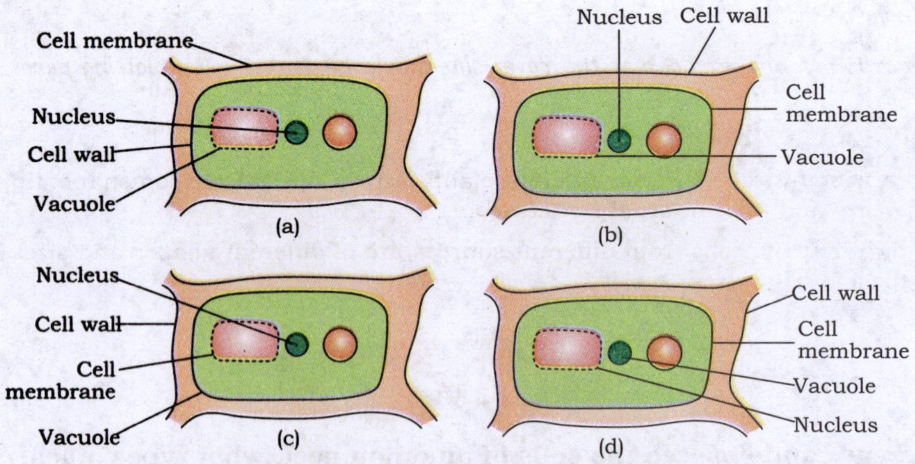


**Ans.** (b)

**Q. 4** **Pick the odd one out. (a) plastids, (b) large vacuole, (c) cell wall (d) centrioles**

**Ans.** (d) Centrioles

# Experiment 4(b)

## AIM

To prepare stained temporary mount of human cheek cells and to record observation and draw labelled diagram.

## Materials Required

A needle, a clean spatula or a toothpick, a brush, slides, cover slips, methylene blue stain, glycerine, a compound microscope and a piece of blotting paper.

## Theory/Principle

The body of all animals, including humans is composed of cells. Unlike plant cells, animal cells do not have cell wall. The outermost covering of an animal cell is a cell membrane. The cytoplasm, nucleus and other cell organelles are enclosed in it.

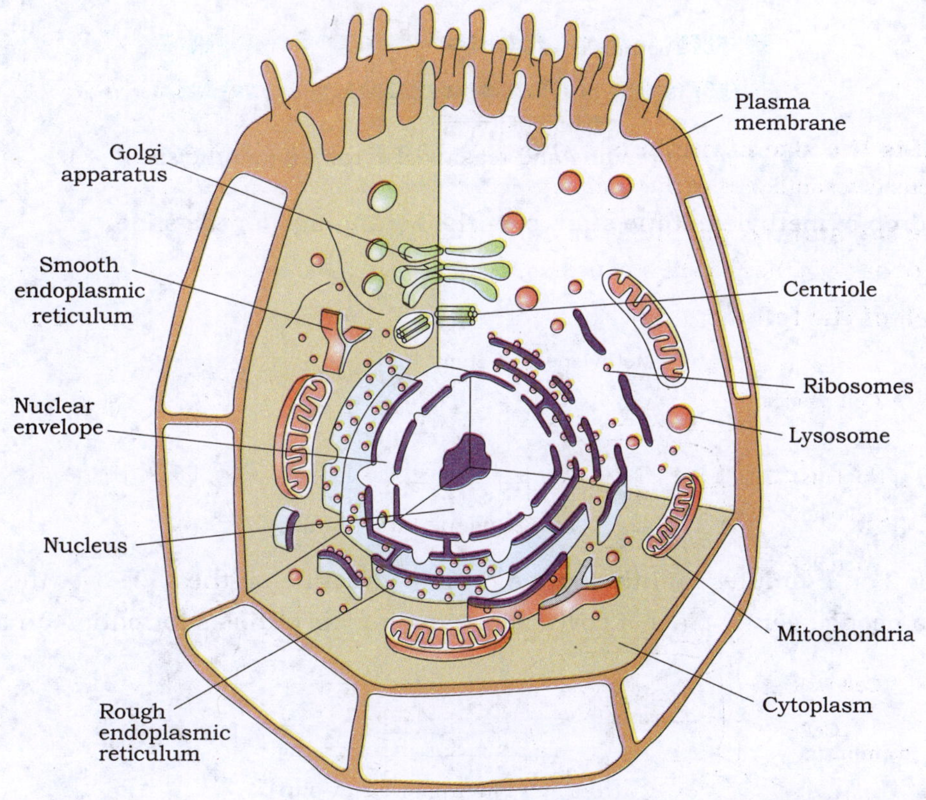


**Fig. 1** A typical animal cell

The outermost covering of most organs and various cavities are formed by epithelial tissue in animals. Cheek cells constitute a type of epithelium tissue called squamous epithelium. These cells are thin, flat and arranged like pavement tiles, i.e. end-to-end forming a delicate lining.

## Procedure (Preparation of Human cheek cells mount)

1. Rinse your mouth with fresh water.
2. With the help of a clean spatula or a toothpick, gently scrap the inner side of your cheek .

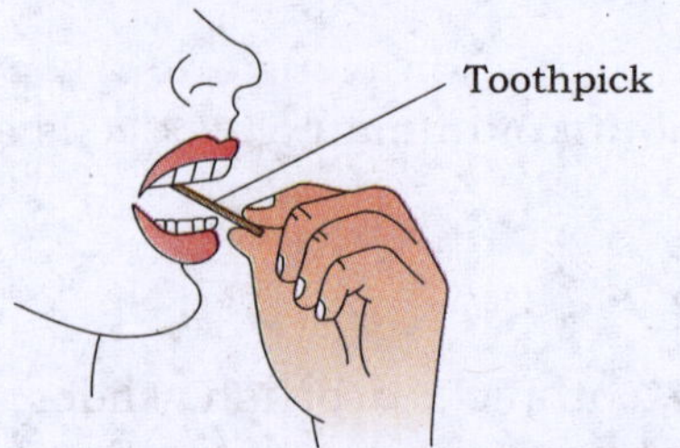


Fig. 2(a) Collecting scrapping from cheek

3. Transfer white pale scrapping into a drop of water taken on a clean slide.
4. Spread the scrappings and tease them with needles to give it a uniform consistency.

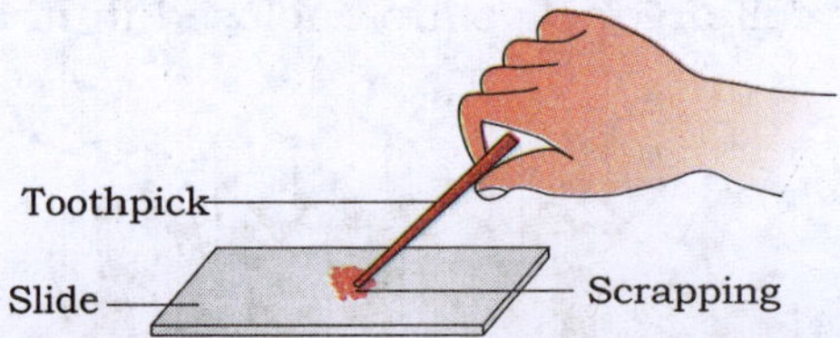


Fig. 2(b) Spreading and teasing of scrapping on the slide

5. Add a drop of methylene blue stain over the scrappings on the slide.

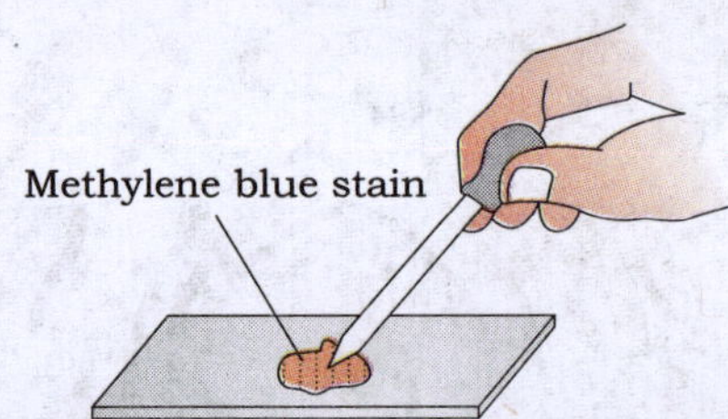


Fig. 2(c) Methylene blue staining

6. Wait for 2 or 3 minutes and then put a drop of glycerine on the slide over the scrappings.
7. Using a needle, gently place a cover slip, avoiding air bubbles formation on the slide .

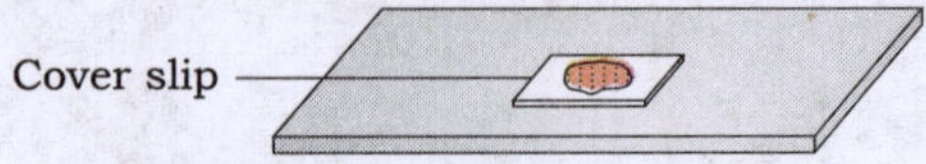


Fig. 2(d) Placing of cover slip

Fig. 2. Preparation of human cheek cells mount

8. By using a blotting paper, remove the excess glycerine from the slide.
9. Examine the slide under microscope, first under low power and then under high power.
10. Draw diagrams of cells as seen under the microscope. Observe and record the features.

## Observations

1. Epithelial cells of human cheek are small, polygonal in shape.
2. Cells are compactly arranged to form a continuous layer.
3. The cells are without cell wall.
4. Cell membrane encloses a distinct nucleus and a vacuole.

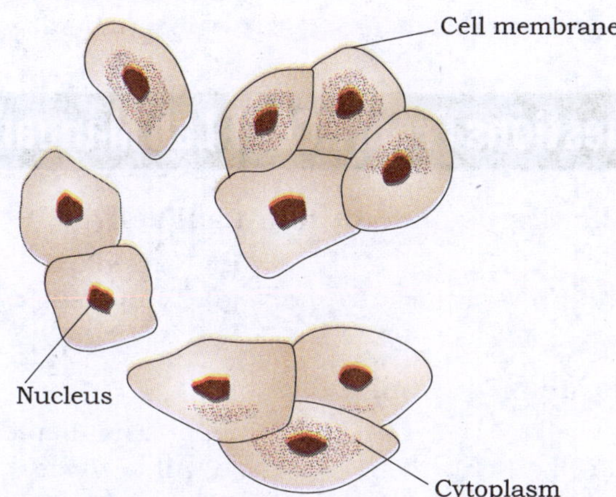


**Fig. 3** Human cheek cells under microscope

### PRECAUTIONS

*1. Scrappings should be removed carefully, avoiding injury to your skin.*

*2. Overstaining is to be avoided. Keep the stain for 2-3 minutes only.*

*3. Care should be taken while placing cover slip to avoid bubbles.*

## Suggested Experiment

Isolate and prepare a temporary mount of plant cells. Note the difference between an **animal cell** and a plant cell and compile a table for same.

**Q. 1 Human cheek cells when observed under microscope will show**

(a) many nucleus in the centre of each cell
(b) a single nucleus in the centre of each cell
(c) no nucleus in the centre of each cell
(d) no cells

**Ans.** (b) a single nucleus in the centre of each cell.

**Q. 2 Where are epithelial cell layer found in our body?**

**Ans.** Epithelial cell layer forms the outer covering of almost all the organs and various cavities of the body.

**Q. 3 An organelle found in plant cells, but absent in animal cells. Name it.**

**Ans.** Chloroplast, it is absent in animal cells.

**Q. 4** **While observing stained cheek cells during the experiment, what would be the colour of**
**(a) Nucleus**
**(b) Cytoplasm?**

**Ans.** (a) Dark blue or black (b) Light blue

**Q. 5** **What cell organelles can be viewed under light microscopes?**

**Ans.** Cell membrane, nucleus and cytoplasm are clearly visible under low power.

## Questions From NCERT Lab Manual

**Q. 1** **Which one of the following is absent in animal cell?**

(a) Cell membrane (b) Nucleolus
(c) Cell wall (d) Cytoplasm

**Ans.** (c) Cell wall is absent in animal cells.

**Q. 2** **Cheek epithelial cells are an example of**

(a) squamous epithelial cells (b) cuboidal epithelial cells
(c) columnar epithelial cells (d) All of these

**Ans.** (a) Squamous epithelial cells

**Q. 3** **Arrange the following steps in correct sequence:**

(i) Putting a drop of glycerine on the cheek cells on a slide.
(ii) Scrapping the inner side of the cheek.
(iii) Adding methylene blue stain.
(iv) Placing the cover slip over the material.

(a) (i), (ii), (iii) and (iv) (b) (ii), (i), (iv) and (iii)
(c) (iv), (ii), (iii) and (i) (d) (ii), (iii), (i) and (iv)

**Ans.** (d) (ii), (iii), (i) and (iv)

**Q. 4** **Name two structures which you would see in cheek cells if you were using a very high magnifying power of microscope.**

**Ans.** Cell membrane and nucleus.

**Q. 5** **Why are cheek epithelial cells always moist?**

**Ans.** These cells are always surrounded by saliva, present inside our mouth, which keeps them moist.

## Practical Based MCQs

*For Experiments 4(a) and 4(b)*

**Q. 1** **Which of the following is called 'powerhouse of the cell' ?**

(a) Mitochondria (b) Ribosome
(c) Lysosome (d) Centriole

**Q. 2** **Which of the following is a single membranous organelle?**

(a) Plastids (b) Mitochondria
(c) Nucleus (d) Lysosome

**Q. 3** **Given below are four diagrams of cells of an onion peel. The correctly labelled diagram is:**

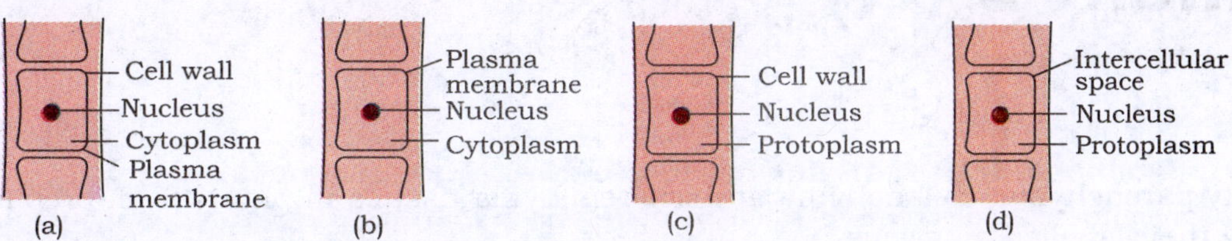


**Q. 4** **The only non-living part of a plant cell is**

(a) endoplasmic reticulum (b) ribosomes
(c) cell wall (d) plasma membrane

**Q. 5** **Which organelle helps in photosynthesis in plant cells?**

(a) Golgi apparatus (b) Ribosomes
(c) Plastids (d) Mitochondria

**Q. 6** **Which of the following pair of organelles is absent in animal cell?**

(a) Plasma membrane and ribosomes (b) Cell wall and mitochondria
(c) Cell wall and plastids (d) Cell wall and vacuole

**Q. 7** **Centrioles are found in**

(a) onion peel cells (b) human cheek cells
(c) plant cells (d) None of the above

**Q. 8** **The inner membrane of mitochondria forms folds called**

(a) cisternae (b) cristae (c) vesicles (d) matrix

**Q. 9** **The growth of cells is regulated by**

(a) mitochondria (b) ribosome (c) nucleus (d) vacuole

**Q.10** **..... cells do not have true nucleus and membrane-bound organelles.**

(a) Eukaryotic (b) Prokaryotic (c) Plant (d) Animal

**Q.11** **Who among the following discovered 'cell'?**

(a) Schwann (b) Robert Hooke (c) Schleiden (d) Virchow

**Q.12** **Which of the following is the largest known cell?**

(a) Onion cell (b) Diatom (c) Cheek cells (d) Ostrich egg

**Q.13** **Choose the smallest known human cell.**

(a) Liver cell (b) Neuron (c) Red blood cell (d) Sperms

## Answers

| | | | | | | |
|---|---|---|---|---|---|---|
| **1.** (a) | **2.** (d) | **3.** (b) | **4.** (c) | **5.** (c) | **6.** (c) | **7.** (b) |
| **8.** (b) | **9.** (c) | **10.** (b) | **11.** (b) | **12.** (d) | **13.** (d) | |

# Experiment 5 (a)

## AIM

To identify parenchyma, collenchyma and sclerenchyma tissues in plants from prepared slides and draw their labelled diagrams.

## Materials Required

Prepared permanent slides of plant tissues (parenchyma, collenchyma and sclerenchyma) and a compound microscope.

## Theory/Principle

A group of cells that are similar in structure and work together to perform a specific function is called a tissue. It can also be defined as a cluster of cells arranged and designed, so as to give the highest possible efficiency of the functions they perform.

There are two types of tissue i.e., plant tissue and animal tissue. Plant tissues are thus broadly classified into meristematic tissue and permanent tissue on the basis of their ability to divide.

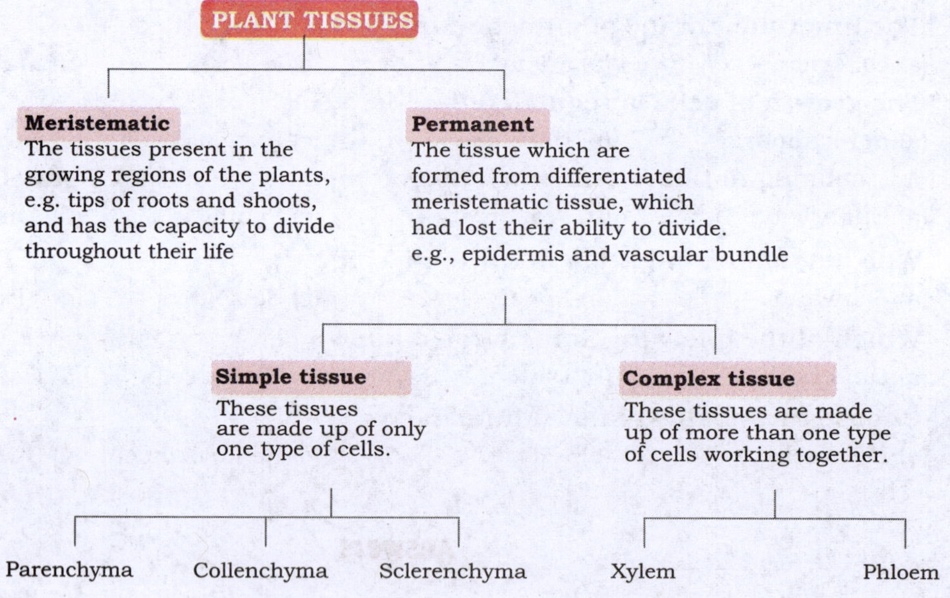


**Fig. 1** Different types of plant tissues

Flowering plants are structurally complex as they are made up of different parts like roots, stems, leaves, flowers, fruits, etc. Each part is an assemblage of different types of tissue and each tissue type has a specific structure and a particular function.

The basic structural features of tissues like cell size, lumen size and cytoplasmic contents are different in different tissues. Parenchyma act as storage tissue for food, air and water. The chlorophyll containing parenchyma are called chlorenchyma. Parenchyma is the most abundant type of tissue in plants.

Collenchyma tissue is found beneath the epidermis of roots and stems. Its function includes protection of the plant against mechanical injury, providing support and flexibility to the growing part of the plant, especially in young stems, petioles and leaves.

Sclerenchyma tissues are composed of dead cells grouped together, having hard and thick walled cells. They provide mechanical strength and protection to the plants, as this tissue is found below the epidermis and around the vascular bundles.

## Procedure

1. Observe the slide of parenchyma tissue (mark it as slide I for reference), collenchyma tissue (side II) and sclerenchyma tissue (slide III), first under the low power of compound microscope.
2. Record the observations for slide I, II and III separately.
3. Change the power of microscope to high and again record the observations carefully.
4. Draw a well labelled diagram of each type of tissue as seen under the microscope.

## Observations

### Slide I (Parenchyma Tissue)

#### Identifying Features

1. The cells of this tissue are isodiametric, oval or round in shape, in transverse section.
2. They have relatively unspecialised cells with thin cell wall.
3. Each cell has a prominently visible nucleus, a large vacuole and peripheral cytoplasm.
4. Intercellular spaces are present in between the cells of parenchyma tissue.

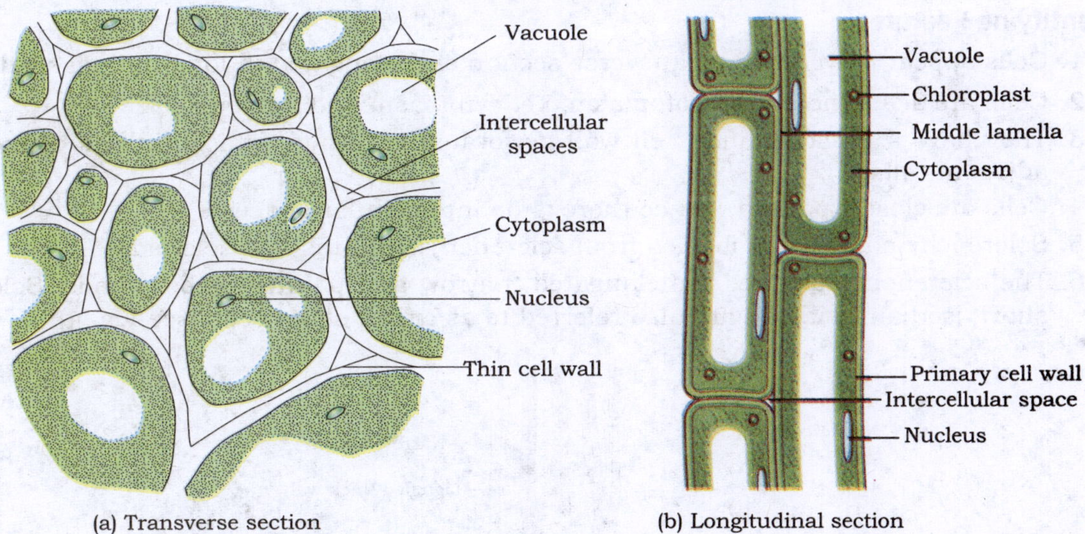


Fig. 2 Parenchyma tissue

## Slide II (Collenchyma Tissue)

### Identifying Features

1. Cells appear oval, spherical or polygonal.

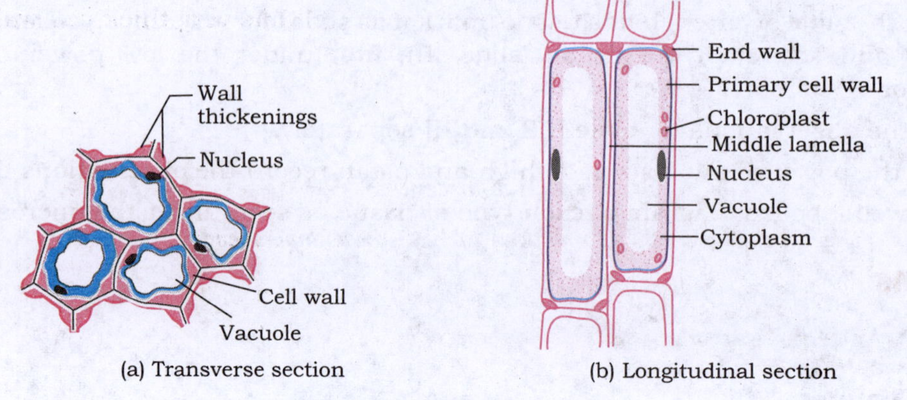


(a) Transverse section (b) Longitudinal section

**Fig. 3** Collenchyma tissue

2. Cells are elastic, living and provide mechanical support.
3. Cells have very little intercellular space.
4. Cell walls of these cells possess thickenings at the corners.

## Slide III (Sclerenchyma Tissue)

### Identifying Features

1. Cells appear polygonal in transverse section and elongated in longitudinal section.
2. Cells are dead and lacks protoplasm, i.e. cytoplasm and nucleus.
3. They have a thick lignified cell wall perforated with pits, which acts as connections to adjacent cells.
4. Cells are closely packed, hence there is no intercellular space.
5. Sclerenchyma tissue is formed from sclerenchyma fibres and sclereids.
6. The sclerenchyma fibres are elongated, narrow and pointed at both ends. Sclereids are short, isodiametric and are also referred to as grit or stone cells (see Fig. 4).

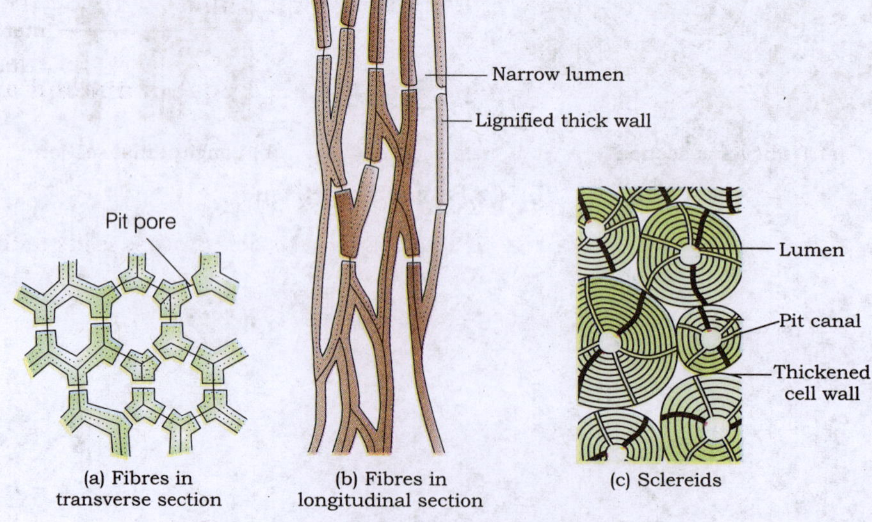


(a) Fibres in transverse section (b) Fibres in longitudinal section (c) Sclereids

**Fig. 4** Sclerenchyma tissue

## Results

Parenchyma are round or oval cells found in stems, leaves, roots, fruits and other soft tissues.

Collenchyma appear polygonal in shape and are of different sizes. These cells are located at the peripheral parts of plant organ, mid ribs of the leaves.

Sclerenchyma are oval, polygonal or of various shapes. Cell has very thick cell wall, nucleus is absent. These cells are present in stiff parts of the plants.

### PRECAUTIONS

1. *Hold the slides by its edges, do not touch it in centre.*
2. *Always view the slide in low power and then in high power microscope.*
3. *Handle compound microscope carefully.*
4. *Draw actual diagrams, as observed under microscope.*

## Suggested Experiments

1. Prepare temporary slides of various parts of the plant, i.e. root, stem and leaves, to study the structure, location and arrangement of various types of cells of permanent tissues in plants.
2. Isolate and study animal cells and tissues. Prepare a report on how plant tissues are different from animal tissues.

## Viva-Voce

**Q. 1 A growing region of a plant will contain which type of tissues?**

**Ans.** Growing region of plants have meristematic tissue, i.e. the cells present in this region retain the property of division throughout their life.

**Q. 2 Name the modification of parenchyma cells which contain chlorophyll.**

**Ans.** Chlorenchyma contains chlorophyll.

**Q. 3 Where is parenchyma found in a plant body?**

**Ans.** In plants, parenchyma forms the major tissue of softer parts like the cortex, pith and leaf mesophyll.

**Q. 4 Mention one identification feature of collenchyma cells.**

**Ans.** The cells are thickened at the corner.

**Q. 5 Name the plant tissue, which is present in the seed coat of almond and makes it very hard.**

**Ans.** Sclerenchyma, mainly sclereids (stone cells) makes seed coat very hard.

**Q. 6 Permanent tissues are unable to divide further. Why?**

**Ans.** Permanent tissues consist of differentiated cells. Differentiation process leads to the cell maturation and assign them specialised functions.

## Questions From NCERT Lab Manual

**Q. 1 In the transverse section of stem which tissue occupies larger space, parenchyma or sclerenchyma?**

**Ans.** Parenchyma occupies larger space.

**Q. 2 Which tissue, when matured, has dead cells?**

**Ans.** Sclerenchyma has dead cells.

**Q. 3 Mention the main function of sclerenchyma tissue.**

**Ans.** Sclerenchyma provides mechanical support and strength to the plant.

**Q. 4 You can bite fruits like guava, grapes, banana etc. but not a piece of wood. Why?**

**Ans.** Fruits like guava, grapes, banana have soft tissue fibres. The wood has hard tissue fibres that have bean lignified and the wood becomes hard.

**Q. 5 Draw an outline of the section of stem and indicate the regions where parenchyma and sclerenchyma are situated.**

**Ans.**

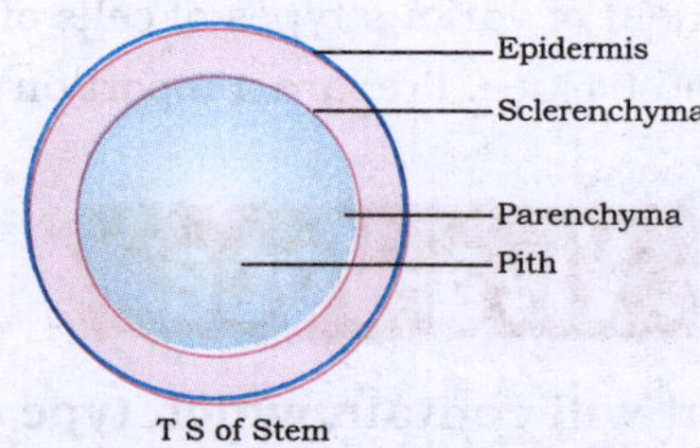


T S of Stem

# Experiment 5 (b)

## AIM

To identify different types of animal tissues (striped muscles fibres, smooth muscle fibres, cardiac muscle fibres and nerve cells) from prepared slides and draw their labelled diagrams.

## Materials Required

Prepared slides of striated muscle, smooth muscle, cardiac muscle nerve cells and a compound microscope.

## Theory/Principle

Like plants, animal body is also made up of group of similar cells, performing specific function, i.e. tissues. In animals there are four basic types of tissues (see Fig. 1) which are composed of different types of cells.

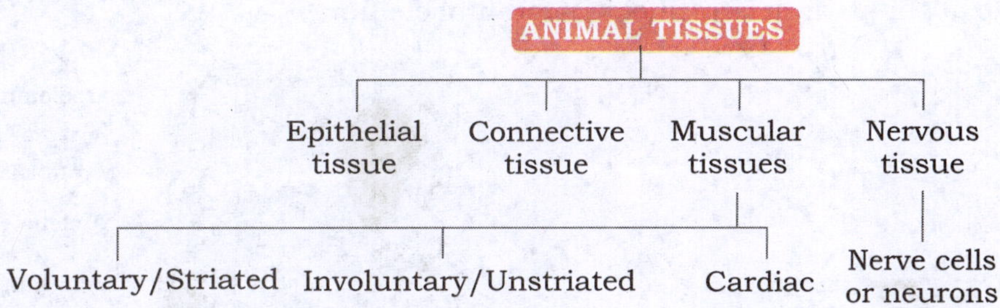


**Fig. 1** Different types of animal tissues

These tissues vary from each other not only in their structures, but also in their functions. Striated muscles are voluntary as they are under the control of the nervous system. These muscles are attached to the bones, hence called skeletal muscles and are found in arms, legs, etc. Striated muscles are not used continuously because they get tired when overworked. Unstraited muscles, also known as smooth muscles are involuntary, i.e. they are not under the control of nervous system. These muscles are found in the iris of the eye, alimentary canal, blood vessels, in ureters and in bronchi of the lungs. They are also responsible for slow rhythmic movement of stomach, intestine and other internal organ.

Cardiac muscles are also involuntary muscle. These muscles form a network in the walls of the heart. They contract rapidly and rhythmically, without fatigue.

The nervous tissue is composed of nerve cells or neurons. These are the longest cells in the body. They are found spread in the entire body and regulates their action by coordinating with the brain. Nerve cells work by sending nerve impulse from axon of one neuron to the dendrites of another neuron through a synapse.

## Procedure

1. Observe the slide A for striated muscles, slide B for smooth muscle, slide C for cardiac muscle fibres and slide D for nerve cells first under low power of microscope.
2. Record your observations for slide A, B, C and D separately.
3. Change the power to high and again observe all the slides.
4. Record the observations carefully.
5. Draw a well labelled diagram of cells of each tissue as seen under the microscope.

## Observation and Result

### Slide A

It shows striated muscle fibres:

1. The muscle fibres are long, cylindrical and unbranched.
2. These fibres show alternate light (thin filaments) and dark bands (thick filaments) or transverse striations.
3. Each muscle fibre is multinucleated, i.e. many nuclei are observed along the fibre resulting from the fusion of many muscle cells. Such a condition is referred as syncytium.
4. Nuclei lie at the periphery of the striated muscle fibre.

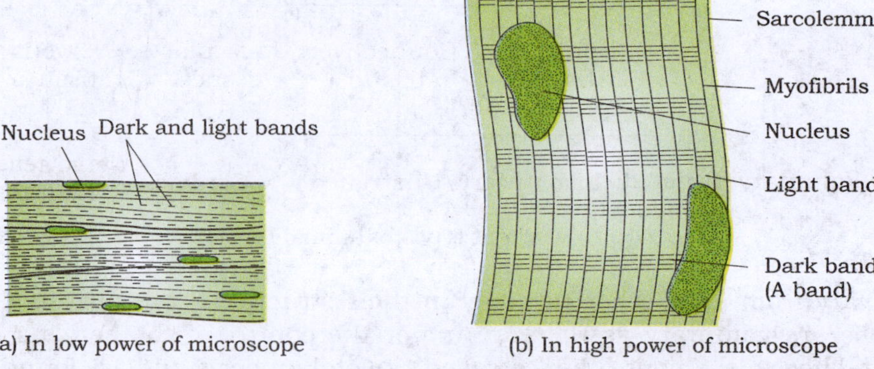


**Fig. 2.** Striated muscle fibre

### Slide B

It shows smooth muscle fibres.

1. These muscle cells are spindle-shaped and are arranged in bundles.
2. Each muscle cell has a homogenous cytoplasm bounded by plasmalemma.
3. In cytoplasm, there are numerous myofibrils, which do not show light and dark bands.
4. Each muscle cell is uninucleated.

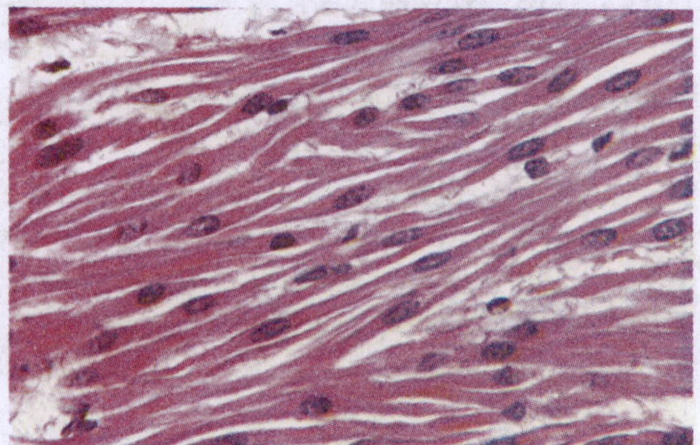

**Fig.3 (a)** Microscopic view of a smooth muscle cells (fibres)

## Slide C

It shows cardiac muscle fibres.

1. Cytoplasm is more abundant and myofibrils show faint striations.
2. Each muscle cell is uninucleated with a centrally located nucleus.
3. Muscle fibres are characterised by the presence of intercalated discs at the junction of two cardiac muscle cells.
4. They have abundant blood supply.

**Fig. 3(b)** Microscopic view of a smooth cardiac muscles

## Slide D

It shows a nerve fibre or neuron.

1. A typical nerve cell or neuron has three main parts
   (a) Cell body or cyton
   (b) Axon
   (c) Dendrites
2. Cyton or the cell body has a prominent nucleus and cytoplasm.
3. The cytoplasm contains granules which are called Nissl's granules.
4. The cell body gives out several branches called dendrons, these further divides into small thread-like structures called dendrites.
5. Axon is the long, cylindrical branch projecting from cell body. It is covered with myelin sheath in some thus called myelinated neuron.
6. Nodes of Ranvier are found in the interrupted spaces or gaps in the axon where myelin sheath is not continuous.

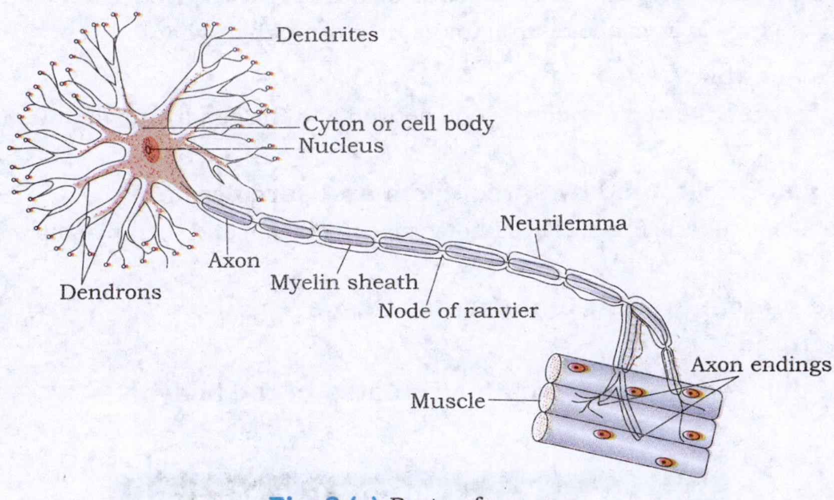


**Fig. 3 (c)** Parts of neuron

PRECAUTIONS

1. Handle the prepared slides carefully.
2. Use microscope with care.
3. Observation should be done first in low power than in high power objective.

## Suggested Experiment

Find more about the other types of tissues present in animals apart from nervous tissue and muscular tissue. Explain their functions and draw the labelled diagrams of each.

## Viva-Voce

**Q. 1 Name the parts of our body containing (a) nerve cells (b) striated muscle.**

**Ans.** (a) Nerve cells – In brain and spinal cord.

(b) Striated muscles – In arms and legs.

**Q. 2 What are the characteristic of a nerve cell?**

**Ans.** A typical nerve cell consists of cell body or cyton, axon and dendrites.

**Q. 3 What is the function of dendrites and axon in the nerve cell?**

**Ans.** The dendrites receive impulses and take them towards the cell body. Axon takes impulses away from the cell body, towards the nerve endings.

**Q. 4 Name the branch of science which deals with the study of cells and tissues.**

**Ans.** Histology is the branch of science (biology) dealing with the study of cells and tissues.

**Q. 5 How does a nerve impulse travel from one neuron to the next?**

**Ans.** Nerve impulse travels from one neuron to the next through a synapse.

**Q. 6 What is a synapse?**

**Ans.** The space between the nerve ending of one neuron and the dendrite of another neuron is called synapse.

**Q. 7 What do you understood by sarcoplasm and sarcolemma?**

**Ans.** The cytoplasm of muscle fibre cells is known as sarcoplasm and their plasma membrane is called as sarcolema.

**Q. 8 Name the protein present in muscular tissue.**

**Ans.** Actin and Myosin.

**Q. 9 Name a fiuid, except flood, which circulates in the body.**

**Ans.** Lymph.

## Questions From NCERT Lab Manual

**Q. 1 What are the features of striated muscle fibre? Where do we find these in our body?**

**Ans.** Striated muscle fibres have strips, i.e. alternating light and dark bands. These are under the control of an organism's will. These muscles are found attached to bones.

**Q. 2 Mention the function of skeletal muscles in our body.**

**Ans.** Skeletal muscles help in the movement of the body parts, bones, joints and our body as a whole.

**Q. 3 What are the features observed in a neuron?**

**Ans.** (i) Longest cell in the body.

(ii) Cell body gives rise to small branches called dendrites.

(iii) A single prominent nucleus is present in the cell body.

## Practical Based MCQs

*For Experiments 5(a) and 5(b)*

**Q. 1 A student was observing a slide. He observed long unbranched cells with striations and many nuclei. The slide may be of**

(a) sclerenchyma (b) striated muscles (c) parenchyma (d) nerve cell

**Q. 2 Which of the following tissues are dead?**

(a) Parenchyma (b) Collenchyma (c) Sclerenchyma (d) All of these

**Q. 3 Name the tissue which makes the plant hard and stiff.**

(a) Collenchyma (b) Sclerenchyma (c) Parenchyma (d) All of these

**Q. 4 Identify the part labelled as '*C*' in the given diagram.**

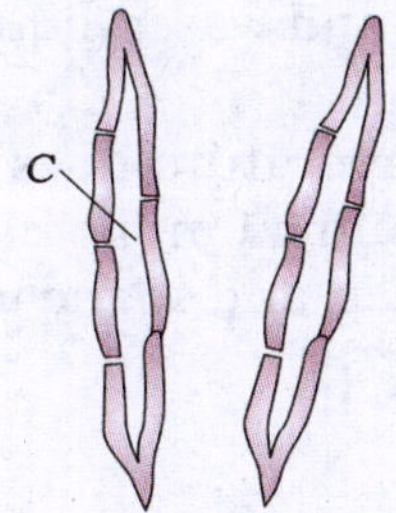


(a) Intercellular space (b) Lumen (c) Pits (d) Sclereids

**Q. 5 Identify the tissue (A) and (B).**

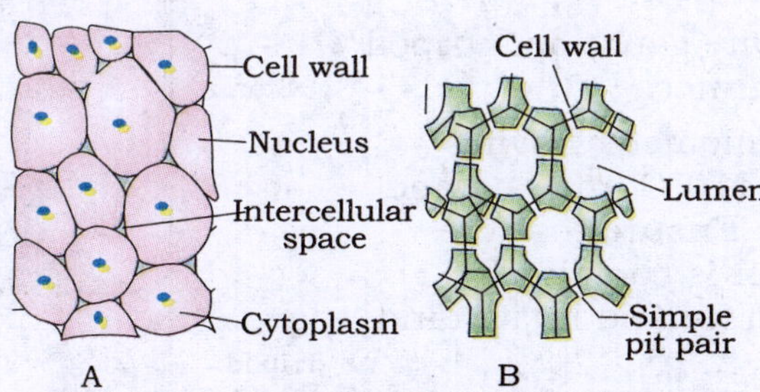


(a) A — Parenchyma tissue ; B — Collenchyma tissue

(b) A — Collenchyma tissue ; B — Sclerenchyma tissue

(c) A — Sclerenchyma tissue ; B — Collenchyma tissue

(d) A — Parenchyma tissue ; B — Sclerenchyma tissue

**Q. 6 Muscles involved in movement of arm are**

(a) cardiac muscles (b) smooth muscles

(c) striated muscles (d) non-striated muscles

### Answers

| 1. | (b) | 2. | (c) | 3. | (b) | 4. | (b) | 5. | (d) | 6. | (c) |
|---|---|---|---|---|---|---|---|---|---|---|---|

# Experiment 6 (a)

## AIM

To determine the melting point of ice.

## Materials Required

Ice (crushed), beaker (100 mL), water, thermometer, water bath, burner, glass rod stirrer, tripod stand and wire gauze iron stand.

## Theory/Principle

The process in which a solid on heating, changes into a liquid is called **melting** or **fusion**. The temperature at which a solid substance gets converted into a liquid, is called the **melting point** (or melting temperature). The melting point may also be called the fusion point or fusion temperature. The melting point of ice is 0°C or 273 K.

$$\text{Ice} \underset{\text{Cool}}{\overset{\text{Heat}}{\rightleftharpoons}} \text{Water (at melting point, 0°C)}$$

At the melting point, both ice (solid state) and water (liquid state) exist together. Below 0°C, only ice exists. Above 0°C, only water exists.

When a solid melts into a liquid, its temperature does not increase even on heating because whole of the supplied heat energy is consumed in increasing potential energy of the molecules. The kinetic energy does not increase further, and so the temperature does not increase as long as the melting continues.

## Procedure

1. Take about 200 g of crushed ice and put it in a clean glass beaker. Place a glass rod in the beaker to stirr the ice.
2. Place the beaker on a wire gauze on a tripod stand over a Bunsen burner.
3. Suspend a celsius thermometer having calibration of –10°C to 110°C from a stand such that it dips in ice. Ensure that the bulb of the thermometer is completely surrounded by crushed ice and let it stand in a vertical position.
   (Note the range and least count of thermometer).
4. Observe the temperature as shown on the thermometer. The temperature will drop till it reaches 0°C.

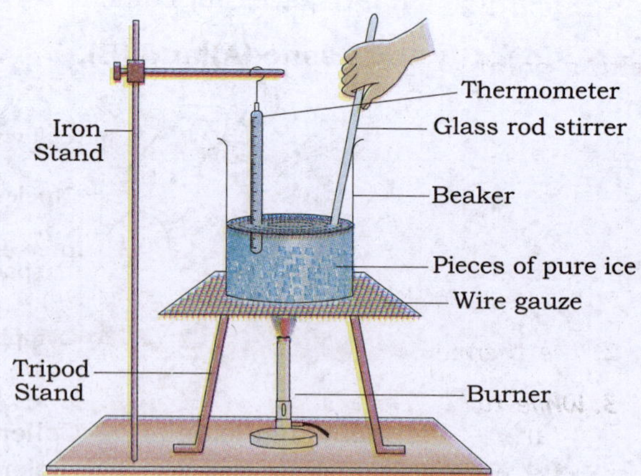


**Fig. 1** Determination of the melting point of ice

5. Light the Bunsen burner and heat the beaker and ice slowly and keep stirring with the glass rod (as shown in Fig. 1).
6. After every one minute, observe the ice and record the temperature on the thermometer.
7. Note the temperature when whole of the ice has been converted into water. Record this temperature of conversion of ice (solid) into water liquid.

## Observation Table

When ice starts changing to water, the temperature is 0°C.

1. The thermometer records temperature as being constant for atleast 2 minutes at 0°C.
2. When ice has completely changed to water, only then does the temperature rise on further heating of water.

Temperature and time data for determining the melting point of ice.

| S. No. | Time (min) | Temperature (°C) |
|---|---|---|
| 1. | 0.0 | ....... |
| 2. | 1.0 | ....... |
| 3. | 2.0 | ....... |
| 4. | 3.0 | ....... |
| 5. | 4.0 | ....... |
| 6. | 5.0 | ....... |
| 7. | 6.0 | ....... |
| 8. | 7.0 | ....... |
| 9. | 8.0 | ....... |
| 10. | 9.0 | ....... |
| 11. | 10.0 | ....... |
| 12. | 11.0 | ....... |
| 13. | 12.0 | ....... |
| 14. | 13.0 | ....... |
| 15. | 14.0 | ....... |

**Note** Total number of observations depends on the conditions of experiment.

## Result

Melting point of ice = .........°C or .........K.

**Note** The melting point of pure ice under standard conditions is taken as 0°C. However, it may change due to impurities in ice and atmospheric pressure.

### PRECAUTIONS

1. *Immerse only the bulb of the thermometer in the crushed ice.*
2. *The thermometer should not touch the wall of the beaker.*
3. *While taking the reading on the thermometer, keep your eye at the level of mercury thread.*
4. *Recording of temperature and time should be done simultaneously.*
5. *Ice should be dry before using for melting point determination.*
6. *Maintain a uniform temperature by continuous stirring.*

## Suggested Experiments

1. Determine the melting point of ice on addition of non-volatile solute, i.e. common salt in it.
2. Determine the melting point of ice on addition of non-volatile solute, i.e. sugar in it.

## Viva-Voce

**Q. 1 What will be the direction of heat flow when a hot solid is put into the beaker containing water at room temperature?**

**Ans.** The direction of heat flow from the hotter to the cold body.

**Q. 2 What is the least count of a thermometer which has 20 graduations between 10°C and 20°C marks?**

**Ans.** 20 graduations indicate 10°C range of temperature, so least count = $\frac{10}{20}$ = 0.5°C.

**Q. 3 If a thermometer is kept in the ice, what does its reading show?**

**Ans.** When a thermometer is kept in the ice, the reading shows that the temperature first decreases and then remains constant at 0°C.

**Q. 4 At room temperature, a student sets up an apparatus to determine the melting point of ice. He takes the beaker half-filled with ice and dips a mercury thermometer in it. What according to you, would he observe?**

**Ans.** He would observe that temperature falls, reaches 0°C and remains constant only as long as both ice and water are present in it.

**Q. 5 What is melting point?**

**Ans.** The temperature at which a solid changes into liquid at atmospheric pressure is called its melting point.

**Q. 6 What happens to the temperature of ice during melting?**

**Ans.** It remains constant at 0°C until all ice has melted.

**Q. 7 Does the melting point depend on atmospheric pressure.**

**Ans.** Yes, the melting point can vary slightly with changes in external pressure.

**Q. 8 Why do we use a beaker instead of a test tube in this experiment?**

**Ans.** A beaker provides a larger surface area for uniform melting and better thermometer placement.

## Question From NCERT Lab Manual

**Q. 1 Why does the temperature remain unchanged until the entire solid changes into liquid even if we are heating the solid?**

**Ans.** Heat is supplied which is used up in the form of latent heat of fusion. The heat is used to overcome the forces of attraction between the molecules and does not indicate a rise in temperature. Hence, temperature remains constant during change of state.

# Experiment 6 (b)

## AIM

To determine the boiling point of water.

## Materials Required

Distilled water, round-bottom flask, a double bored cork, thermometer, iron stand, sand bath, tripod stand, stopwatch, bent tube, wire gauze, burner, pumice stone, beaker or porcelain pieces.

## Theory/Principle

**Boiling** is a physical process that takes place at a constant temperature during which the matter changes from liquid to vapour state.

$$\text{Water} \underset{\text{Cool}}{\overset{\text{Heat}}{\rightleftharpoons}} \text{Water vapour}$$

The **boiling point** of the liquid is a measure of the forces of interaction occurring between the molecules of the liquid. When a liquid (such as water) is heated, its molecules gain energy and their kinetic energy increases. On continuous heating, a particular temperature is reached when these molecules leave the surface (in the form of vapour) to produce a pressure above the liquid equal to the atmospheric pressure. At this stage, the temperature remains stationary even on further heating.

The stationary temperature at which the pressure of the vapours leaving the surface of the liquid equals the atmospheric pressure is called the **boiling point** of the liquid.

## Procedure

1. Take about 100 mL of distilled water and put it in a clean round-bottom flask.
2. Put 2-3 pieces of pumice stone or porcelain pieces in the above flask. Place the flask on a wire gauze on a tripod stand over a Bunsen burner.
3. Close the mouth of the flask with a two bore cork, such that a celsius thermometer (having calibration from –10°C to 110°C )is fitted in one bore, and a right-angled delivery tube is fitted in the other bore.
4. Ensure that bulb of the celsius thermometer does not dip in water, but is atleast 5 cm above the level of water in the flask.
5. Record the temperature on the thermometer.
6. Place a small beaker under the other end of the delivery tube to collect the condensed water (as shown in Fig. 1).
7. Light the Bunsen burner and heat the water in the flask, on slow heat. Record the temperature at regular intervals, as the water gets heated, till it begins to boil.
8. Allow the steam to pass through the delivery tube and condense in the beaker.

9. Record the temperature on the thermometer after every 1 minute intervals, after the water begins to boil.

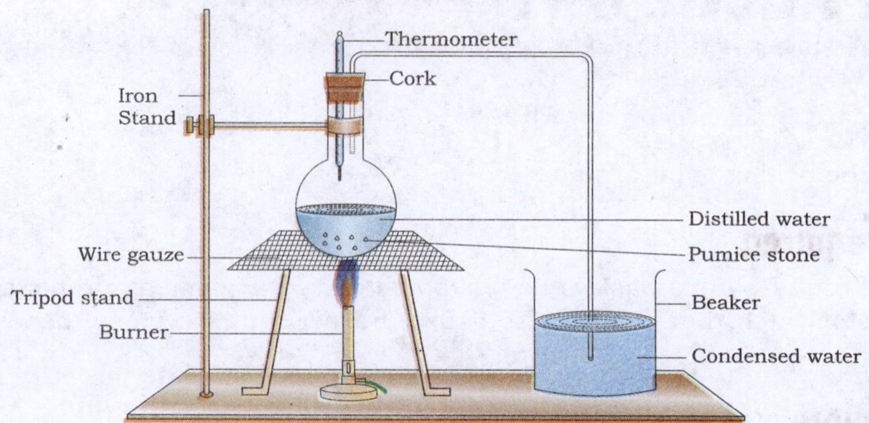


**Fig. 1** To determine boiling point of water

## Observation Table

1. The thermometer records temperature as being constant for at least 2 minutes at 100°C.
2. During any change of state, temperature of the substance remains constant.

Thus, during boiling of water, the temperature of water will remain constant at its boiling point. Therefore, from the values given in table.

**Temperature time data for determining the boiling point of water**

| S.N. | Time (min) | Temperature (°C) | S. No. | Time (min) | Temperature (°C) | S. N. | Time (min) | Temperature (°C) |
|---|---|---|---|---|---|---|---|---|
| 1. | 0 | ....... | 6. | 5 | ....... | 11. | 10 | ....... |
| 2. | 1 | ....... | 7. | 6 | ....... | 12. | 11 | ....... |
| 3. | 2 | ....... | 8. | 7 | ....... | 13. | 12 | ....... |
| 4. | 3 | ....... | 9. | 8 | ....... | 14. | 13 | ....... |
| 5. | 4 | ....... | 10. | 9 | ....... | 15. | 14 | ....... |

**Note** Total number of observations depends on the conditions of experiment.

## Result

Boiling point of water = .........°C or ......... K.

**Note** The boiling point of water under standard conditions is taken as 100°C. However, it may differ due to impurities in water and atmospheric pressure.

### PRECAUTIONS

*1. In the case of boiling point determination, the bulb of the thermometer should be kept outside the water.*

*2. Add porcelain pieces before heating to avoid bumping.*

*3. Heat water by rotating the flame.*

*4. Note the temperature by keeping the eyes in the line with the level of mercury.*

*5. Use distilled water only. Impure water and hard water have boiling point greater than 100°C.*

*6. Recording of temperature and time should be done simultaneously.*

## Suggested Experiments

1. Determine the boiling point of water if some non- volatile solute (common salt) is added in it.
2. Determine the boiling point of hard water and compare it with boiling point of distilled water.

## Viva-Voce

**Q. 1 Generally when a liquid is to be boiled, we place a few pieces of porcelain in the flask. Why is this done?**

**Ans.** Porcelain pieces are placed in the flask containing a liquid to be boiled to prevent bumping of the liquid.

**Q. 2 Why is a bent tube provided in the cork set into the mouth of a distillation flask?**

**Ans.** When the water starts boiling, the steam, if not allowed to go out will increase pressure on the surface of water. This will cause an increase in the boiling point. The delivery tube allows the excess steam to go out and maintain pressure equal to the atmospheric pressure inside the flask.

**Q. 3 A thermometer has 20 equal divisions between 90℃ and 100℃ marks. A student while determining the boiling point of water finds that the mercury thread becomes stationary at the 19th mark above 90℃. What should he record as the boiling point of water?**

**Ans.** 20 divisions indicate 10°C range of temperature so, least count $= \frac{10}{20} = 0.5°$ C and temperature at the 19th mark above 90°C will be $100°C - 1 + 0.5°C = 99.5°C$

**Q. 4 What happens to the boiling point of a liquid when some impurities are added to it?**

**Ans.** After adding impurities to a liquid, its boiling point changes. The changes depend upon the nature of impurities. If the impurities are volatile, then boiling point decreases and if they are non-volatile, then boiling point increases.

**Q. 5 What changes can be seen when thermometer bulb is dipped below the surface of water while determining boiling point of water?**

**Ans.** Correct reading is not shown by thermometer as boiling point is affected by the pressure (volume of water).

**Q.6 As water boils at 100°C when atmospheric pressure is 1 atm, why is it so?**

**Ans.** It is so because, when atmospheric pressure is 1 atm, then the vapour pressure of a liquid equals the atmospheric pressure at 100°C and hence, water boils.

**Q.7 What is boiling point?**

**Ans.** The temperature at which the vapour pressure of a liquid becomes equal to the atmospheric pressure and the liquid starts boiling.

**Q.8 What is the boiling point of pure water?**

**Ans.** Boiling point of pure water is 100°C or 373.15 K at 1 atmospheric pressure (760 mm Hg).

## Questions From NCERT Lab Manual

**Q. 1 Why is the bulb of thermometer kept above the surface of water while determining the boiling point of water?**

**Ans.** Bulb of thermometer is kept above the surface of water while determining the boiling point of water because steam contains only water vapour and the effect of any non-volatile impurity (if present) will be nullified.

**Q. 2 Why do we fix a two holed cork in the round bottom flask while determining the boiling point of water?**

**Ans.** One hole of the cork is to fix the thermometer in such a way that the bulb of the thermometer does not touch the bottom or sides of the flask and second hole is to fix a delivery tube to allow the vapours to escape.

## Practical Based MCQs

*For Experiments 6(a) and 6(b)*

**Q. 1 Which of the following is the correct method of finding the melting point of ice?**

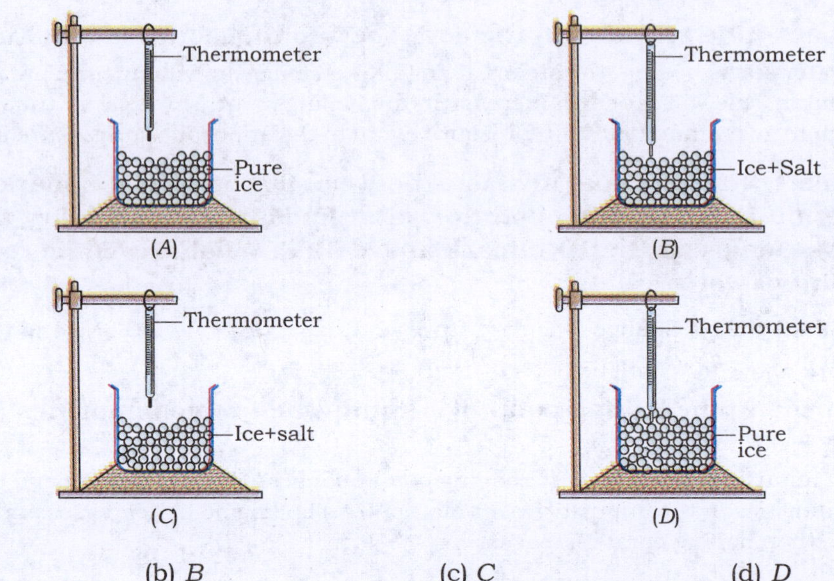


(a) *A* (b) *B* (c) *C* (d) *D*

**Q. 2 In an experiment to determine the melting point of ice, Rakshita observes no change in the temperature, when she heats the ice till the whole ice melts. The reason of no rise in temperature could be that the heat supplied to ice**

(a) is used to change the ice from its solid state to liquid state.
(b) goes to the surroundings and is not absorbed by the ice.
(c) has no effect on temperature because ice is very cold.
(d) goes to the beaker in which it is kept.

**Q. 3 When ice melts, cooling is produced because of one of the following :**

(a) Density of ice is less than water.
(b) Ice floats on water.
(c) Ice absorbs heat from the surroundings.
(d) Melting point of ice is 0°C.

**Q. 4 In the determination of melting point of ice, correct reading of melting point is noted in the thermometer when**

(a) temperature starts rising.
(b) temperature becomes constant.
(c) ice starts melting.
(d) whole of the ice gets melted.

**Q. 5 Water in a container is heated uniformly from 0° C to 100° C. The temperature**

(a) increases continuously.
(b) decreases continuously.
(c) decreases upto 4°C and increases further.
(d) increases upto 4°C and decreases further.

**Q. 6 Which one of the following would not be required for the determination of melting point of ice?**

(a) Thermometer (b) Iron stand (c) Pumice stone pieces (d) Stirrer

**Q. 7 While heating a liquid, it has to be stirred properly. This is to let**

(a) the dust particles not settle at the bottom.
(b) the liquid get uniform temperature throughout.
(c) the liquid get heated quickly.
(d) the liquid evaporate faster.

**Q. 8 When a thermometer is kept in the ice, the reading shows that**

(a) temperature keeps increasing.
(b) temperature keeps decreasing.
(c) temperature increases first and then decreases.
(d) temperature first decreases and then remains constant at 0° C.

**Q. 9 In an experiment to determine the boiling point of water, the stopwatch used to note down the temperature of water at different intervals of time has 20 divisions between 0 to 10 s marks. The least count of the stopwatch is**

(a) 1s (b) 0.1 s (c) 0.05 s (d) 0.5 s

**Q.10 You are given ice at –10° C. It is supplied with heat at a constant rate. The temperature of ice changes with the heat supplied. Which of the following graph describes the correct observations?**

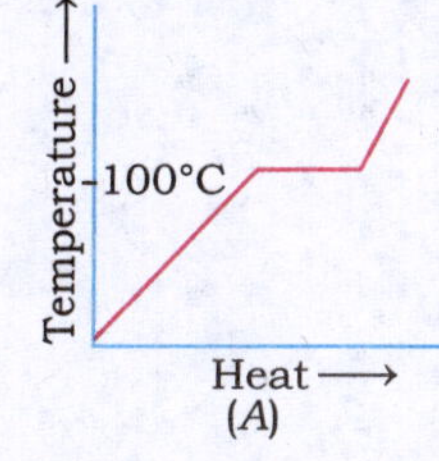

(A)

Temperature ⟶
100°C
Heat ⟶
(B)

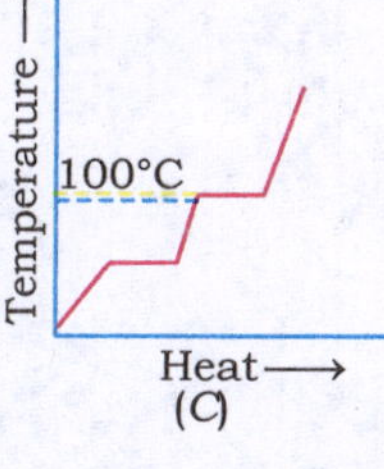

(C)

Temperature ⟶
100°C
Heat ⟶
(D)

(a) *A* (b) *B* (c) *C* (d) *D*

**Q.11 Liquid *A* boils at 60℃, while liquid *B* boils at 80° C. Which is more volatile?**

(a) Liquid *A* (b) Liquid *B* (c) Both *A* and *B* (d) Neither *A* nor *B*

**Q.12 Reema, Archana, Shakti and Anu made the arrangements I, II, III and IV respectively for the determination of boiling point of water. Which one of them has made the correct set up?**

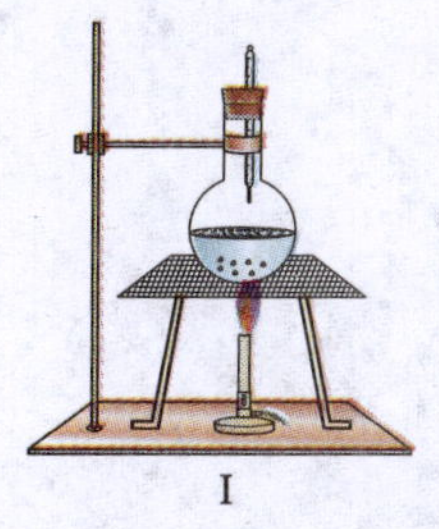
I

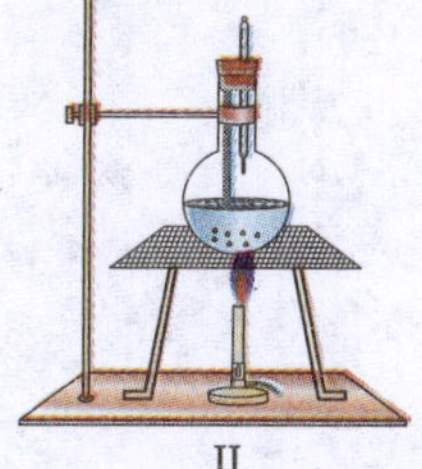
II

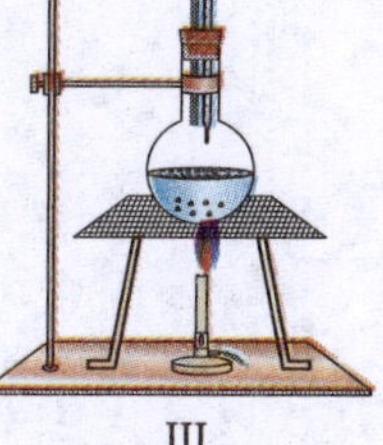
III

IV

(a) I (b) II (c) III (d) IV

**Q.13 Which of the following set of apparatus is required to determine the boiling point of water?**

(a) Funnel, burner, clamp, stand, test tube, thermometer and wire gauze

(b) Tripod stand, conical flask, thermometer, wire gauze, stand with clamp and pair of tongs

(c) Boiling tube, beaker, thermometer, burner, cork with one hole, stand with clamp and wire gauze

(d) Round bottom flask, burner, thermometer, wire gauze, stand with clamp, cork with two holes and glass tube

**Q.14 Prakhar set up an apparatus for the determination of boiling point of distilled water at Shimla. He recorded the boiling point as 97 °C, instead of 100° C. Assuming that the thermometer is accurate, the lesser boiling point is due to**

(a) high pressure of air at high altitude.

(b) low pressure of air at high altitude.

(c) water may be containing a large amount of dissolved air.

(d) the water may not be distilled.

## Answer

| | | | | | | | | | | | |
|---|---|---|---|---|---|---|---|---|---|---|---|
| **1.** | (d) | **2.** | (a) | **3.** | (c) | **4.** | (b) | **5.** | (c) | **6.** | (c) |
| **7.** | (b) | **8.** | (d) | **9.** | (d) | **10.** | (c) | **11.** | (a) | **12.** | (c) |
| **13.** | (d) | **14.** | (b) | | | | | | | | |

# Experiment 7

## AIM

To verify the laws of reflection of sound.

## Materials Required

A meter scale, two identical metallic pipes of length 1 m and of diameter 10 cm, a protractor and a source of low amplitude sound such as a table clock.

## Theory/Principle

Sound is a longitudinal wave that propagates in the form of compressions and rarefactions in the medium. It is the form of energy which gives us sensation of hearing. It is produced by vibrating bodies only. It requires a material medium for propagation.

As light ray (electromagnetic wave) gets reflected when it falls on a smooth surface and follows laws of reflection. Similarly, sound wave also follows laws of reflection.

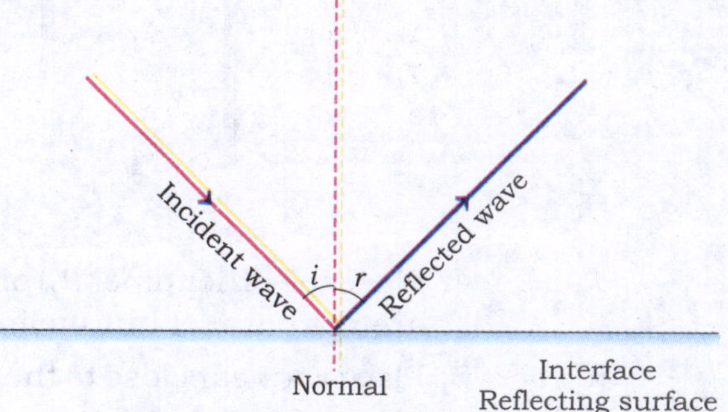

**Fig. 1** Reflection of sound wave

### Laws of Reflection of Sound

1. The incident sound wave, the reflected sound wave and the normal to the surface all lie in the same plane (see Fig. 1).
2. The angle of incidence ($\angle i$) is always equal to the angle of reflection ($\angle r$) (see Fig. 1).

### Speed of Sound

It depends on the nature of the medium through which the waves pass. Presence of moisture increases the velocity of sound in air, because the density of dry air is greater than the density of moisture.

Speed of sound in air (at normal temperature and pressure) is 344 m/s. When we rise the temperature, speed of sound increases and *vice-versa.*

### Some Important Points Regarding Sound Waves

- Pitch, intensity and quality are the three main characteristics of sound.
- Sound waves produce an echo. Which is the repetition of the original sound heard after reflection from an object. Echo can only be heard, if the reflected sound reaches the ear after $\frac{1}{10}$th of a second.
- The production of multiple echoes are called reverberations.
- To hear an echo, minimum distance between the source of sound and reflecting surface should be 17.2 m.

## Procedure

**A. Angle of incidence ($\angle i$) = Angle of reflection ($\angle r$)**

1. Take two pipes, $P_1$ and $P_2$.
2. Place one of the pipes $P_1$ on the table top, inclined to the wall with its one end near the wall.
3. Place the table clock close to the other open end of the pipe ($P_1$) as shown in Fig. 2. Also, place a piece of cardboard along the normal, which will acts as a screen.

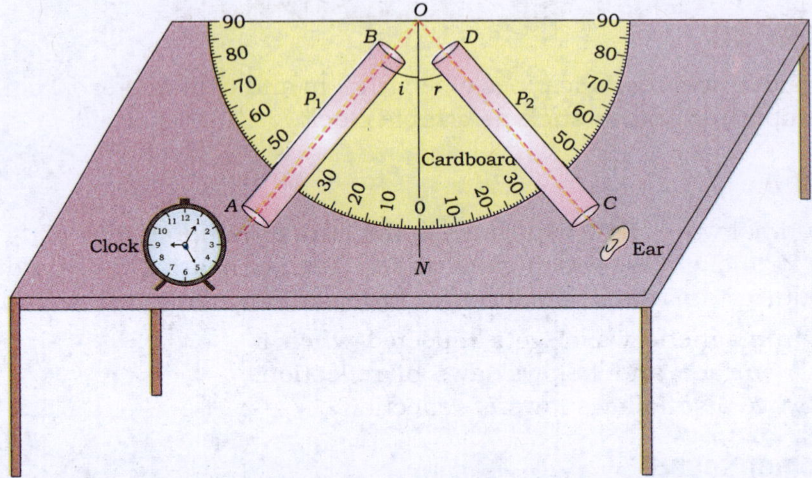


**Fig. 2** Experimental set up

4. Place the other pipe ($P_2$) on the table, almost at the same inclination with wall. The two pipes are not parallel but inclined towards each other.
5. Place your ear close to the other open end of pipe $P_2$ and try to hear the sound of the clock.
6. Adjust the inclination of the pipe $P_2$ on the table top such that the sound of clock is very clearly heard.
7. With the help of chalk piece, draw lines *AB* and *CD* along the lengths of the pipes $P_1$ and $P_2$ respectively.
8. Remove the pipes and extend the lines *AB* and *CD* towards the wall. They will meet at a point *O* at the edge of the table touching the wall. Sound gets reflected from the wall at this point.
9. Draw a normal *ON* at the point *O* perpendicular to the edge of the table.
10. Measure the angle $\angle AON$ and $\angle CON$, i.e. angle of incidence ($\angle i$) and angle of reflection ($\angle r$) respectively, using the protractor.
11. Repeat this experiment with two more different inclinations of the pipe $P_1$ with the wall.
12. Record the observations.

**B. The incident sound wave, the reflected sound wave and the normal to the surface all lie in the same plane.**

13. Repeat the steps 1 to 6.
14. When the sound is best heard through the pipe $P_2$, lift the pipe a slightly vertically upwards, you will find that sound is no longer heard clearly. The reason for this is that now, the incident sound wave, the reflected sound wave and the normal to the surface, all lie in the same plane.

## Observation Table

| S. No. | Angle of incidence ($\angle i = \angle AON$) | Angle of reflection ($\angle r = \angle CON$) |
|---|---|---|
| 1. | | |
| 2. | | |
| 3. | | |

## Results

1. When the pipe $P_2$ (through which sound is heard) is lifted vertically or obliquely, then the sound of clock either weakens or diminishes completely. It shows that the reflected wave should lie in the same plane of incidence, which verifies first law of reflection of sound.
2. The angle of incidence and the angle of reflection of sound are found to be equal, which verifies second law of reflection of sound.

### PRECAUTIONS

1. *The inner surface of metallic tube should be highly polished.*
2. *Watch or clock used should be in good working condition.*
3. *Tuning fork or clock should be close to the tube, but it should not touch the tube.*
4. *There should be complete silence in the laboratory so that sounds from other sources do not interfere.*

## Sources of Error

1. Measurements of angles should be done by taking the axes of the pipes as the incident and reflected rays.
2. You should take care in placing the two pipes and in drawing lines *AO* and *BO*.
3. As we are dealing with relatively larger dimensions, so a bigger protractor is to be used.
4. A larger amplitude sound source can make you hear the sound directly from source and not after reflection from the wall travelling through pipes.

## Suggested Experiments

1. Perform the same experiment, when whole set-up is immersed in water and discuss the result.
2. Find out how can you increase the velocity of sound with respect to air. Explain why sound cannot travel in vacuum.

## Viva-Voce

**Q. 1 What type of wave is sound?**

**Ans.** Sound is a longitudinal wave that can only propagate through a material medium.

**Q. 2 Curtains and other thick materials such as fibreboards, etc., are used in a laboratory. Why?**

**Ans.** Curtains and other thick materials are used in laboratory to absorb echoes and get soothing sound.

**Q. 3 What is the speed of sound in air at normal temperature and pressure?**

**Ans.** Speed of sound in air is 344 m/s.

**Q. 4 What is the use of placing a cardboard between the two pipes?**

**Ans.** It does not allow the direct hearing of the sound of the clock.

**Q.5 Give the range of audible frequency of sound.**

**Ans.** The range of audible frequency of sound is 20 Hz to 20000 Hz.

**Q.6 What will be the angle of reflection of sound wave, if it falls perpendicular to a reflecting surface?**

**Ans.** As from the question, angle of incidence is zero, so angle of reflection will be zero.

**Q.7 Can any hard and plane surface serve as a reflector of sound waves?**

**Ans.** Yes, any hard and plane surface can serve as a reflector of sound waves because the wavelength of sound wave is very large as compared to the wavelength of light wave.

**Q.8 What changes are observed in a medium through which a longitudinal wave propagates?**

**Ans.** During the propagation of longitudinal wave, volume and density of the medium change.

**Q.9 State whether the method of using ear as a receiver is always accurate or not.**

**Ans.** It may not always be an accurate method, because the perception of the observer can varies.

**Q.10 What happens to the speed of sound as temperature increases?**

**Ans.** The speed of sound increases with increase in temperature.

## Questions From NCERT Lab Manual

**Q. 1 While performing this experiment, why do we prefer to use pipes of larger length but of smaller diameter?**

**Ans.** In reality, sound source cannot produce a ray of sound instead it produces beam of sound in all directions, so to avoid unwanted sound, it is advised to take the pipes of larger length and smaller diameter.

**Q. 2 How the experiment of reflection of sound is different from the experiment on laws of reflection of light?**

**Ans.** As we know that, reflection of light involves smooth and polished surface but for reflection of sound, reflecting surface may be polished or rough.

**Q. 3 Which sheet will you choose as sound reflecting surface for this experiment**
**(a) a smooth wooden board or**
**(b) a thermocol sheet?**

**Ans.** We should preferably use a smooth wooden board because it reflects most of sound waves. However, thermocol sheet absorbs most of sound waves because it is good absorber of sound.

**Q. 4 Suppose the whole experimental set up of this experiment is submerged in water. What changes do you expect in observations?**

**Ans.** As the speed of sound in water is much faster than air, so the reflected sound will be heard faster but angle of incidence remains equal to the angle of reflection.

**Q. 5 Why do we require a low amplitude sound source in this experiment?**

**Ans.** For a high amplitude sound source, we hear the sound directly from sound source, so it will be difficult to observe the reflected sound wave, hence we need a low amplitude sound source.

**Q. 6 What alterations can be made in the pipes to make the reflected sound more distinct and clear?**

**Ans.** As we know that, the rough surface is good absorber of sound waves. So to have reflected sound more clear and distinct, a layer of newspaper may be inserted into the pipes.

## Practical Based MCQs

**Q. 1 The correct position of the ear of the observer is shown in**

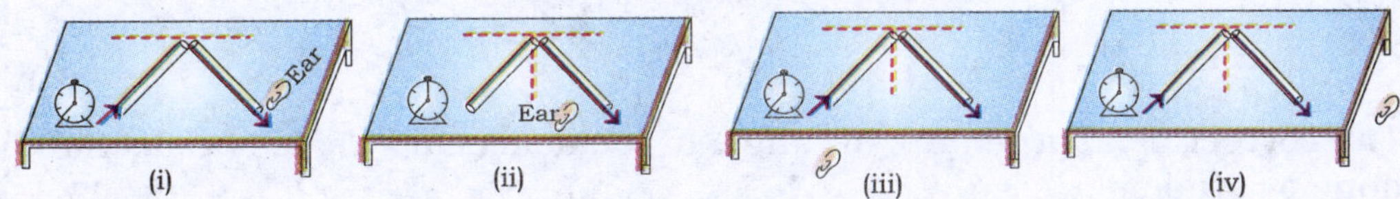


(a) Only Fig. (i)
(b) Only Fig. (ii)
(c) Fig. (iii) and (iv)
(d) All of these

**Q. 2 Two students while performing experiment on verification of laws of reflection of sound are provided with the following choices**
**(i) Using a narrow tube or wide tube.**
**(ii) Using a faint source of sound or strong source of sound.**
**The best results would be obtained by the student using the combination of**

(a) narrow tube and faint source of sound
(b) narrow tube and strong source of sound
(c) wide tube and faint source of sound
(d) wide tube and strong source of sound

**Q. 3 While performing the experiment on reflection of sound, the incident sound is directed along**

(a) axis of tube
(b) normal to the axis of tube
(c) at an angle of 30° from the axis of the tube
(d) at an angle of 45° from the axis of the tube

**Q. 4** **Ramjeet, while verifying the laws of reflection of sound measured the angle between the incident sound wave and reflected sound wave to be 130°. The angle of incidence will be**

(a) 65° (b) 55° (c) 45° (d) 60°

**Q. 5** **Reflection of sound wave requires**

(a) transparent surface (b) opaque surface
(c) translucent surface (d) None of these

**Q. 6** **In which medium, the reflection of sound does not occur?**

(a) Air (b) Water
(c) Vacuum (d) None of these

**Q. 7** **When the sound wave propagates, which physical quantity changes in the medium?**

(a) Only pressure (b) Only density
(c) Both density and pressure (d) Only frequency

**Q. 8** **While doing the experiment on reflection of sound, plane or hard wooden surface can serve as a**

(a) reflector of sound wave (b) absorber of sound wave
(c) emitter of sound wave (d) None of the above

**Q. 9** **While doing experiment on verifying the law of reflection of sound, four students measured the angles $\angle i$ and $\angle r$ as shown in the diagram.**

I II III IV

**The correct measurements of angle of incidence and angle of reflection has been done by student**

(a) I (b) II (c) III (d) IV

**Q.10** **While doing the experiment reflection of sound, the sound received in the ears is**

(a) the direct sound from clock (source)
(b) sound coming through the tube after reflection
(c) the sound reflected from any reflector
(d) None of the above

**Q.11** **Sound wave is also known as**

(a) a transverse wave (b) a longitudinal wave
(c) a tidal wave (d) None of these

**Q.12** **Short duration wave is also called**

(a) a pulse (b) a wave
(c) a pair of waves (d) a train of pulse

## Answers

| | | | | | |
|---|---|---|---|---|---|
| **1.** (a) | **2.** (a) | **3.** (a) | **4.** (a) | **5.** (b) | **6.** (c) |
| **7.** (c) | **8.** (a) | **9.** (a) | **10.** (b) | **11.** (b) | **12.** (a) |

# Experiment 8

## AIM

To determine the density of solid (denser than water) by using a spring balance and a measuring cylinder.

## Materials Required

Measuring cylinder (100 to 200 mL), a piece of cotton thread, a spring balance, water and a piece of solid which is to be experimented.

## Theory/Principle

The mass occupied by the unit volume of a substance is called its **density**. It is denoted by ρ.

Mathematically, $$\rho = \frac{M}{V}$$

where, $M$ = mass of the body (i.e. the amount of matter contained in a substance)

$V$ = volume of the substance

The SI unit of density is $kg/m^3$. Density is the physical property of matter that describes the close packing of individual particles in a substance. Density of the most substances decreases with rise in temperature.

**Densities of some common substances**

| Substances | Density ($kg\ m^{-3}$) |
|---|---|
| Air | 1.30 |
| Ice | 920 |
| Water | 1000 |
| NaCl (common salt) | 2160 |
| Iron | 7800 |
| Silver | 10500 |
| Gold | 19300 |

### Spring Balance

Spring balance is the instrument used to measure the weight/ force of the substance by which it is attracted towards centre of the earth.

### Working principle of spring balance

**According to Hooke's law, the extension produced in a spring is directly proportional to the force applied (i.e. weight of the body) on the spring (see Fig. 1) of a spring balance.**

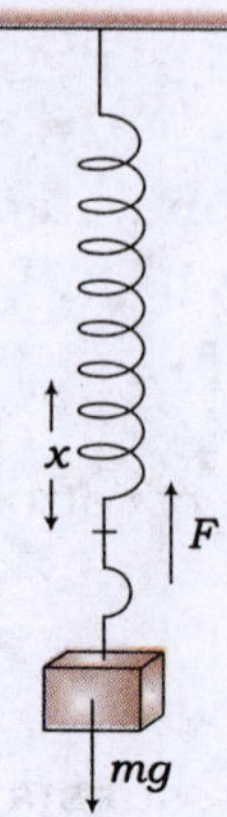


**Fig. 1** Stretched of spring of distance x from its equilibrium position

$$F = -kx = mg$$

**where, $k$ = spring constant,**

**$m$ = mass of the substance and**

**$g$ = acceleration due to gravity**

### Graduated cylinder

**It is a measuring cylinder marked with scale in mL or in cubic centimetres (cc). It is used to measure the volume of liquid.**

## Procedure

**This experiment can be completed in two steps:**

### A. Measuring the mass of the solid by using spring balance

1. **Take spring balance capable of weighing upto 100 g.**

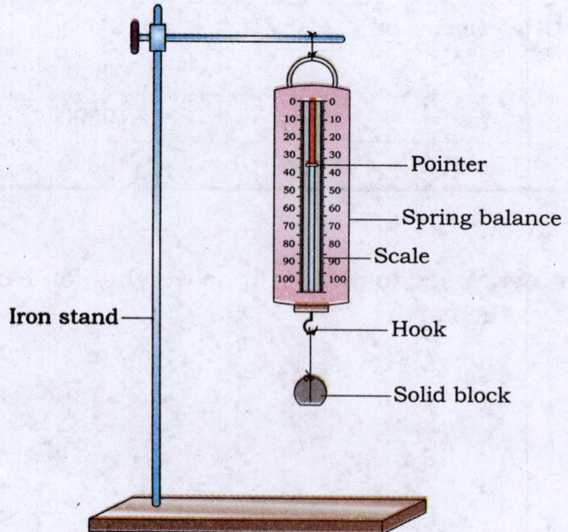


**Fig. 2** Determination of mass of the solid using spring balance

2. Hang the spring balance vertically on an iron stand and note down the position of its pointer on the scale.
3. Check the spring balance for zero error and find its least count and record it.

$$\text{Least Count} = \frac{\text{Range of spring balance}}{\text{Total number of divisions}}$$

4. Tie the metallic solid block with the cotton thread and hang it with the lower hook of spring balance (see Fig. 2).
5. Note down the pointer reading of the spring balance.
6. Repeat the process two or three times and record the observations in the observation table.

## B. Measuring the volume of the solid block using measuring cylinder

1. Note down the least count of the measuring cylinder. For a 100 mL capacity cylinder, usually the least count is 1 mL.
2. Pour some water into the measuring cylinder and place it on a table.
3. Note the level of water in the cylinder by reading the lower meniscus.
4. Hang the solid block with the help of a thread gently into the water so, that it is completely immersed in water (as shown in Fig. 3).
5. Note down the new water level reading.
6. Take difference between the two readings gives the volume of the solid block.
7. Repeat the experiment atleast three times.
8. Record your observations in a tabular form.

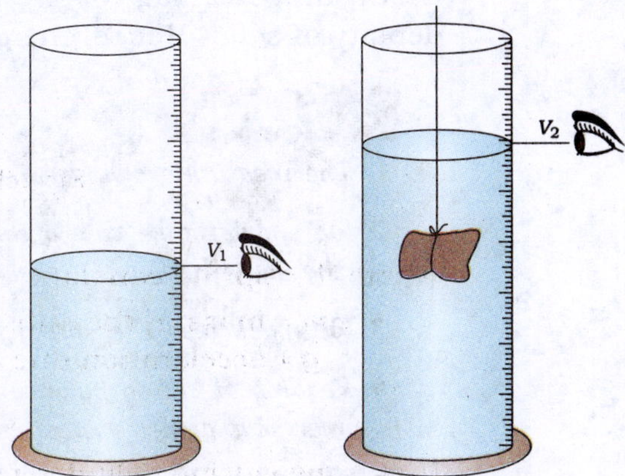

**Fig. 3** Eye kept at level of water

## Observations

1. Least count of the spring balance = ... gf
2. Zero error of the spring balance = ... gf

### A. Weight of the given solid block

| S.No. | Initial reading of spring balance (without block), $w_i$ (gf) | Final reading of spring balance (with block), $w_f$ (gf) | Weight of the block, $w_f - w_i$ (gf) |
|---|---|---|---|
| 1. | | | |
| 2. | | | |
| 3. | | | |

### B. Reading of water level in measuring cylinder

Least count of measuring cylinder = ... mL

| S.No. | Initial level of water ($V_i$) (mL) | Final level of water ($V_f$) (mL) | Volume of solid block ($V_f - V_i$) (mL) |
|---|---|---|---|
| 1. | | | |
| 2. | | | |
| 3. | | | |

## Calculations

1. Mean weight of solid block, $w = \dfrac{w_1 + w_2 + w_3}{3} = \ldots$ gf

2. Mass of solid block, $m = \ldots$ g

3. Mean volume of solid block, $V = \dfrac{V_1 + V_2 + V_3}{3} = \ldots.$ mL

4. Density of solid block = $\dfrac{\text{Mean mass of solid block}}{\text{Mean volume of solid block}} = \dfrac{m}{V}$ g/mL $= \dfrac{m}{V} \times 1000$ kg/m$^3$

## Result

On dividing the mass of given solid by its measured volume from measuring cylinder, we get the density of solid. Hence, the density (ρ) of the solid substance will be ...... kg/m$^3$.

### PRECAUTIONS

1. The measuring cylinder used must be dry and clean.
2. We should take care of line of sight while taking the reading of measuring cylinder. It must be at the same horizontal level as that of lowest meniscus.
3. We must keep the spring balance vertical while taking the weight of solid.
4. Reading of spring balance and graduated measuring cylinder should be taken when the pointer and meniscus comes to rest, respectively.
5. The solid substance must be dried and wiped carefully before repeating the experiment.
6. The pointer of the spring balance should move freely on the scale.
7. The solid block should be fully immersed in water and should not touch the sides and bottom of measuring cylinder.

## Sources of Error

1. Markings on the measuring cylinder and on spring balance may not be uniform.
2. Least count of both the instruments must be taken before carrying out any measurement.
3. Cotton thread can absorb water.

## Suggested Experiments

1. Can you suggest an experiment to determine the density of solid (less denser than water)?
2. By doing an activity, show that what happens when a porous solid is used to carry out this experiment.

## Viva-Voce

**Q. 1 Name the device which is used to measure mass and the weight of an object.**

**Ans.** Mass is measured using a physical balance, and weight is measured using a spring balance.

**Q. 2 Can you give the difference in mass and weight of a body?**

**Ans.** **Mass** is a measurement that refers to the amount of matter that makes up an object and is measured in kilogram (kg).

**Weight** is the force by which mass is attracted towards the centre of earth is called its weight and is measured in newtons (N).

**Q. 3 A body has mass equal to 1000 g. What will be the weight of the body?**

**Ans.** As we know, weight of the body is equal to the force by which its mass is attracted towards centre of the earth.

So, $F = mg$ [where, $m$ = mass and $g$ = acceleration due to gravity = 9.8 $m/s^2$]

$F = 1 \text{ kg} \times 9.8 = 9.8 \text{ N}$ $[\because 1000 \text{ g} = 1 \text{ kg}]$

**Q.4 How will you calculate the volume of solid dipped in water?**

**Ans.** The volume of a solid is calculated by subtracting the initial water level from the final water level after dipping the solid in a measuring cylinder.

**Q.5 Which water has higher density, river or salt water?**

**Ans.** Salt water has more density than river water.

**Q.6 How will you manage the error in the measurement of volume of water in measuring cylinder?**

**Ans.** We can minimise the error by taking a graduated measuring cylinder having a scale of smallest least count.

**Q.7 What are the two forces which will decide whether a body can sink or float?**

**Ans.** Gravitational force and buoyant force.

**Q.8 If the solid (heavier than water) is soluble in water, how will you find its volume by a measuring cylinder?**

**Ans.** Instead of water, we can use kerosene oil or any other liquid in which solid is insoluble for measuring its volume.

**Q.9 Is there any effect of temperature on density?**

**Ans.** Yes, density decreases with rise in temperature as with rise in temperature, volume of the body increases.

**Q.10 Why one should use dry measuring cylinder for performing the experiment to determine the density of a solid by using a spring balance and a measuring cylinder?**

**Ans.** The measuring cylinder should be dry and without any liquid, since it will change the volume or weight of liquid.

**Q.11 When will a body sink?**

**Ans.** When the density of the body is greater than the density of the liquid or weight is more than buoyant force, body will sink.

**Q.12 Mention any two precautions that should be taken while determining the density of a solid by using spring balance.**

**Ans.** Two precautions are given below

(i) Spring balance should be sensitive enough to detect small variations and should be error free.

(ii) The measuring cylinder should be clean and dry, since it will change the volume or weight of the liquid.

## Questions From NCERT Lab Manual

**Q.1 Can you determine the density of a porous solid by using a spring balance and a measuring cylinder? Give reasons in support of your answer.**

**Ans.** No, we cannot determine the density of porous solid by using a spring balance and a measuring cylinder because the porous solid will absorb some water which can change its weight and volume of water displaced by it.

**Q.2 How does the presence of an air bubble in the liquid taken in the measuring cylinder affect the volume of solid?**

**Ans.** As we know that, the presence of air bubble in the water increases the volume of water in cylinder, so ultimately the apparent change in volume gets affected.

**Q.3 Density of a sealing wax is 1. 8 g/cm$^3$, express it in kg/m$^3$.**

**Ans.** Density of wax = $1.8\,g/cm^3 = \frac{1.8 \times 10^{-3}}{(10^{-2})^3} = 1.8 \times 10^3\ kg/m^3$

**Q. 4 A metal cylinder is melted and the whole mass is cast in the shape of a cube. What happens to its density? Give reasons.**

**Ans.** As in this case, mass and volume of the new shape remains same, so there will be no change in the density.

**Q. 5 At which temperature, the density of water is maximum?**

**Ans.** At 4°C, the density of water is maximum. It is due to the anomalous behaviour of water which states that the water at temperature 4°C has maximum density (The density of water at 4°C = 1000 kg/m$^3$).

## Practical Based MCQs

**Q. 1 What happens to the density of water when the temperature fall below 4°C?**

(a) increase
(b) decrease
(c) remain same
(d) first increase and then decrease

**Q. 2 Density of glass is 2.5 g/ cm$^3$. This means**

(a) mass of glass is 2.5 g
(b) volume of glass is 2.5 cm$^3$
(c) 1 cm$^3$ of glass will weigh 2.5 g
(d) None of the above

**Q. 3 Mass of the body = 62.4 g**

(i) Reading of water level in measuring cylinder without solid body ($V_1$) = 16.4 mL
(ii) $V_2$ (with solid body) = 24.4 mL

Based on the above observation, the density of material (in g/cc) is

(a) 7.8 (b) 7.4
(c) 2.56 (d) 3.8

**Q. 4** **Spring balance is based on which principle?**

(a) Extension of spring $\propto$ mass of the body

(b) Extension of spring $\propto \dfrac{1}{\text{mass of the body}}$

(c) Extension of spring $\propto$ stretching force

(d) Extension of spring $\propto \dfrac{1}{\text{stretching force}}$

**Q. 5** **A student notes the mass of a solid as 200 g and volume as 40 $cm^3$. What is the density of the solid?**

(a) 5 $g/cm^3$ (b) 0.2 $g/cm^3$
(c) 80 $g/cm^3$ (d) 160 $g/cm^3$

**Q. 6** **In a spring balance, the space between 0 and 25 g marking is divided into 10 equal parts. What will be the least count of spring balance?**

(a) 0.25 g-wt (b) 2.5 g-wt (c) 250 g-wt (d) 0.025 g-wt

**Q. 7** **If we want to determine the volume of a solid by immersing it in water, what should be the nature of solid?**

(a) The solid should be heavier than water and soluble in it
(b) The solid should be lighter than water and insoluble in it
(c) The solid should be lighter than water and soluble in it
(d) The solid should be heavier than water and insoluble in it

## Answers

| **1.** (b) | **2.** (c) | **3.** (a) | **4.** (c) | **5.** (a) | **6.** (b) | **7.** (d) |
|---|---|---|---|---|---|---|

# Experiment 9

## AIM

To establish the relation between the loss in weight of a solid when fully immersed in

(i) tap water

(ii) strongly salty water, with the weight of water displaced by it by taking atleast two different solids.

## Materials Required

A wooden block, a measuring cylinder 100 mL (must have a least count of about 1 mL), two non-porous solids of different sizes, an overflow-can, fresh water, strongly (concentrated) salty water (known density), a piece of silk thread, spring balance and iron stand.

## Theory/ Principle

When the a solid object is immersed in water below the surface of water, four vertical forces act on the object. These forces can be grouped in two sets:

### (a) Downward forces

(i) The weight of the block.

(ii) The downward thrust due to pressure of liquid on the top surface of the block.

### (b) Upward forces

(i) The tension of the spring (which measures the apparent weight).

(ii) The upward force which acts on an object when it is immersed in a liquid is called **upthrust** or **buoyant force**.

## Pressure

The force acting perpendicularly on a unit area is called pressure.

i.e. $$\text{Pressure } (p) = \frac{\text{Force } (F)}{\text{Area } (A)}$$

SI unit of pressure is $Nm^{-2}$ or pascal (Pa).

Pressure at a point inside the liquid is directly proportional to the height of liquid ($h$), density of liquid ($\rho$) and acceleration due to gravity ($g$).

i.e. $$p = \rho g h$$

## Archimedes' Principle

According to this principle, when a body is immersed partially or fully inside a liquid, the upward force exerted by the liquid on the body is equal to weight of liquid displaced by the body.

This upward force exerted by the liquid is called **buoyant force** or **force of buoyancy**.

In other words, when a body is fully or partially immersed in a liquid, there is apparent decrease in its weight which is equal to the weight of liquid displaced by it.

## Law of Floatation

A body will float if the weight of the body is equal to the weight of the liquid displaced. If the weight of the immersed body is more than the weight of the water displaced, the body will sink.

## Procedure

### A. For tap water

1. First of all, find the range and least count of the spring balance and measuring cylinder.
2. Now, ensure that the vertically suspended spring balance must have pointer at the zero mark.
3. Check the markings on the spring balance, if it is marked in mass then measured mass must be multiplied by acceleration due to gravity (*g*) to calculate its weight.
4. Now tie one of the solids and suspend it vertically downward (as shown in Fig. 1).
5. Note down the reading on the spring balance.

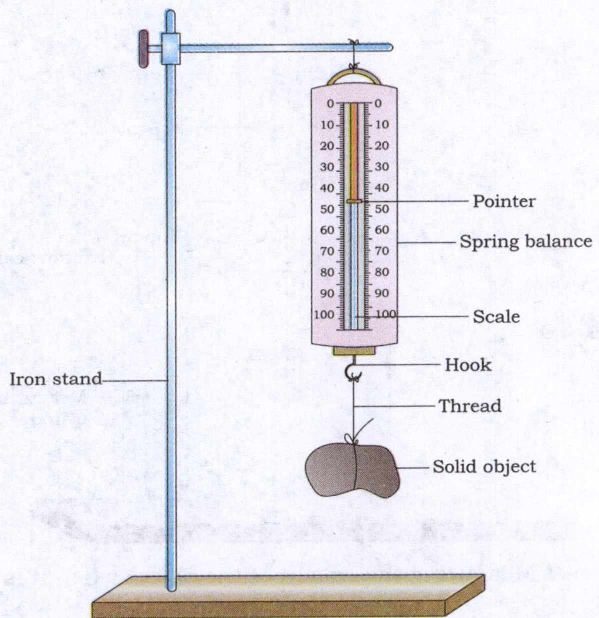


**Fig. 1** Measuring the weight of the object in air

6. Calculate the true weight of the solid in air by subtracting the zero error from the observed weight of the solid in air.
7. Place the overflow-can on the wooden block and slowly pour tap water into it, untill the water just starts overflowing through its spout. At this moment, stop pouring water. After a few moments, the water from the spout stops overflowing. In this situation, the water in the overflow-can is at the verge of overflowing.
8. Place the clean and dry measuring cylinder under the spout of the overflow-can.
9. Now, gently lower the solid (which is suspended from the hook of the spring balance) into the water in the overflow-can till it gets completely immersed. At the same time, the water overflows through the spout and gets collected in the measuring cylinder (as shown in Fig. 2).

10. Read and record the weight of the solid when fully immersed under water by subtracting the zero error from the observed weight.
11. Wait till the tap water stops dripping out from the spout and note down the volume of tap water collected in measuring cylinder.
12. Repeat the process from step 7 onwards for the second solid and record the complete observations.

### B. For strongly salty water

1. Repeat the whole process from step 4 onwards for salty water in the overflow-can.
2. Record the observations in the observation table.

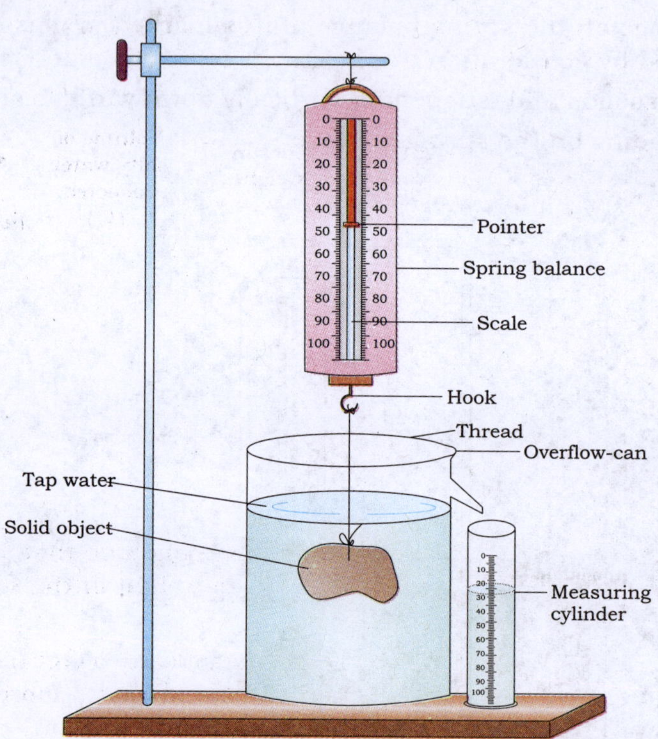


Fig. 2 Measuring the weight of the object when it is immersed in water

## Observations and Calculations

Least count of spring balance = ... N (or gf) or ... g

Zero error in spring balance = ... N or ... g

Acceleration due to gravity ($g$) = 9.8 m/s$^2$

Density of tap water ($\rho_t$) = ........ kg/m$^3$

Density of salty water ($\rho_s$) = ........ kg/m$^3$

## A. For tap water

| S. N. | Solid body | Weight of body in air ($w_a = mg$) | Weight in tap water ($w_t$) | Loss in weight ($\Delta w = w_a - w_t$) | Volume of tap water collected ($V_t$) | | Weight of tap water collected $w_{tc} = V_t \times \rho_t \times g$ | Difference in loss in weight of solid and weight of displaced tap water ($\Delta w \sim w_{tc}$) |
|---|---|---|---|---|---|---|---|---|
| | | (N) | (N) | (N) | mL | $m^3$ | (N) | (N) |
| 1. | First | | | | | | | |
| 2. | Second | | | | | | | |

## B. For strongly salty water

| S.N. | Solid body | Weight of body in air ($w_a = mg$) | Weight in salty water ($w_s$) | Loss in weight ($\Delta w = w_a - w_s$) | Volume of salty water collected ($V_s$) | | Weight of salty water collected ($w_{sc} = V_s \times \rho_s \times g$) | Difference in loss in weight of solid and weight of displaced salty water ($\Delta w \sim w_{sc}$) |
|---|---|---|---|---|---|---|---|---|
| | | (N) | (N) | (N) | mL | $m^3$ | (N) | (N) |
| 1. | First | | | | | | | |
| 2. | Second | | | | | | | |

## Result

According to the above observations and calculations, we conclude that for both the solids and for both the cases(tap water and salty water), the loss in weight of the solids is approximately equal to the weight of liquid displaced by the solids.

It is also observed that the loss in weight is more in case of salty water (i.e. if the density of the liquid is more in which solids are immersed, then the liquid exerts more upward force on the surface of immersed solids).

### PRECAUTIONS

1. Pointer of the spring balance should be set to the zero mark.
2. Spring balance must be hanged vertically.
3. In the overflow-can, the liquid must be filled to the point of just overflowing.
4. Solids used for the experiment must be fully immersed in water.
5. Reading of the spring balance should be taken only when the pointer comes to rest.
6. The solids used should be non-porous.
7. The measuring cylinder must be kept on a horizontal surface, and the observer's line of sight should be at the level of the lower meniscus of water while taking the measurements.
8. There should be no air bubble inside the water.

## Sources of Error

1. Graduation marks may not be evenly spaced.
2. The impurities may alter or change the density of liquid used during experiment.
3. Spilling of liquid, whose weight is to be measured may happen.
4. The thread used to tie the solid object in the experiment may also absorb some water which will cause some error in measurement.

## Suggested Experiments

1. Perform an experiment in which solid used have lesser density than that of liquid.
2. Find out how we can reduce the effect of buoyancy and viscous drag in air.

# Viva-Voce

**Q. 1 Give some of the precautions that must be taken while using an overflow-can.**

**Ans.** The two precautions are as follows

(i) Level of the liquid must be upto the brim.

(ii) All displaced liquid should be collected untill dripping stops.

**Q. 2 State Archimedes' principle.**

**Ans.** It states that the body partially or fully immersed in a liquid experiences an upward force (buoyant force) which is equal to the weight of liquid displaced by the volume of the immersed body.

**Q. 3 Can you explain, what happens when an object of density equal to the density of liquid is dipped?**

**Ans.** If the density of an object is equal to the density of liquid, then it will float on the surface of the remain suspended in the liquid neither shrirking nor floating.

**Q. 4 How can you say that a body experiences loss in weight when fully or partially immersed in a liquid?**

**Ans.** When a body is fully or partially immersed in a liquid, the liquid exerts upward force on the lower surface of solid, due to which body experiences loss in weight.

**Q. 5 Give the name of the forces that act when a body is dipped in liquid partially or fully.**

**Ans.** The forces which act on the body when it is immersed in a liquid partially or fully are as follows

(i) Weight of the body (acts downward)

(ii) Buoyant force (acts upward)

**Q. 6 When a body sinks in a liquid, what happens to the weight of the body?**

**Ans.** A body in a liquid sinks only when the weight of the body is greater than the buoyant force acting on it.

**Q. 7 What are the factors on which buoyant force depend?**

**Ans.** (i) Density of liquid ($\rho$)

(ii) Volume of body immersed ($V$)

(iii) Acceleration due to gravity ($g$) at that place

**Q. 8 Why does the reading on spring balance reduce, when a solid body tied to its hook is fully immersed in water?**

**Ans.** When a solid body tied to the hook of spring balance is fully immersed in water, it experience an upward force called buoyant force or upthrust acts on the solid. As a result, reading on the spring balance reduces.

**Q. 9 Can you tell me any two applications of Archimedes' principle?**

**Ans.** (i) To determine the relative densities of solids and liquids.

(ii) To find the purities of substances, especially expensive substances like gold without harming the item.

**Q.10 What are the two upward forces which act upon a body when immersed partly or completely in water?**

**Ans.** Upward acting forces are as follows

(i) The tension in the spring (which measures the weight).

(ii) The upthrust or buoyant force due to the liquid acting on the lower surface of the body.

## Questions From NCERT Lab Manual

**Q. 1 Why is it easier to swim in sea water rather than a swimming pool or river water?**

**Ans.** As we know that, the density of sea water is greater than the pool water or river water due to which buoyant force acting on the floating body will be greater. So, it is easier to swim in sea water rather than swimming pool/or river water.

**Q. 2 In which liquid– glycerine or kerosene, the loss in the weight of a solid object when fully immersed in it will be more?**

**Ans.** As the density of glycerine as compared to kerosene is more, so the loss in weight of a solid object fully immersed in glycerine will be more.

**Q. 3 How can you perform this experiment for a solid whose density is lesser than that of the liquid used?**

**Ans.** It is done by using a sinker (i.e. another solid body with higher density) to sink it down in the liquid.

**Q. 4 Using this method, how would you find the density of liquid?**

**Ans.** As we know that,

Loss in weight of the solid object = Volume of liquid displaced × density of liquid

= Weight of the liquid displaced

So, $$\text{density } (\rho) = \frac{\text{Weight of liquid displaced}}{\text{Volume of liquid displaced}}$$

**Q. 5 How will you select solid to perform this experiment using glycerine instead of water?**

**Ans.** The solid selected to perform this experiment must have higher density than that of glycerine.

**Q. 6 What are the limitations of this experiment?**

**Ans.** (i) Graduation marks may not be evenly spaced on the spring balance used in this experiment.

(ii) The impurities present in tap water may alter the density of liquid used during this experiment.

## Practical Based MCQs

**Q. 1 An object is immersed in different fluids, the buoyant force acting on it will be**

(a) same

(b) may be same or different

(c) different

(d) does not act at all

**Q. 2** **A solid of density $1 g/cm^3$ is immersed in water, then its**

(a) weight is more than the upthrust
(b) weight is less than the upthrust
(c) weight and upthrust are equal
(d) None of the above

**Q. 3** **When a solid is immersed fully or partially in water, the apparent loss of weight of the solid in water is**

(a) equal to the weight of water displaced by solid
(b) more than the weight of water displaced by solid
(c) less than the weight of water displaced by solid
(d) does not depend on the weight of water displaced by solid

**Q. 4** **When a body immersed in (i) tap water and (ii) salty water, the upthrust on a body in tap water and salty water are denoted by $U_A$ and $U_B$ respectively, then**

(a) $U_A = U_B$ (b) $U_A > U_B$ (c) $U_A < U_B$ (d) $U_A = 2U_B$

**Q. 5** **A man adds salt to water present in a bucket, it will**

(a) increase its density (b) not affect its density
(c) decrease its density (d) increase and decrease sometimes

**Q. 6** **When a body is immersed in a liquid, in which direction the buoyant force acts on the body?**

(a) Vertically upward direction (b) Vertically downward direction
(c) Both (a) and (b) (d) None of these

**Q. 7** **Name the physical quantity in which apparent loss is observed when a solid object is immersed in a liquid.**

(a) Force (b) Upthrust (c) Pressure (d) Density

**Q. 8** **While performing the experiment 'Archimedes principle' Rama took a glass stopper of $10 cm^3$ volume and observed its weight as 40 g-wt. using a spring balance, then, she immersed the glass stopper completely in tap water. What will be the weight of glass stopper?**

(a) 25 g-wt (b) 30 g-wt (c) 20 g-wt (d) 40 g-wt

**Q. 9** **When a body sinks in a liquid, the weight of the body is**

(a) more than buoyant force (b) less than buoyant force
(c) equal to buoyant force (d) None of these

**Q.10** **If the density of the object placed in a liquid is equal to the density of the liquid, the object will**

(a) float (b) sink
(c) float wholly immersed (d) float partly immersed.

**Q.11** **The buoyant force on an object submerged in a fluid depends on**

(a) the object's density (b) the fluid's density
(c) the acceleration due to gravity (d) Both (b) and (c)

**Q.12** **The density of a block of wood which floats with 0.2 of its volume above water is**

(a) $0.8 g/cm^3$ (b) $0.6 g/cm^3$
(c) $1 g/cm^3$ (d) $1.2 g/cm^3$

## Answers

| | | | | | |
|---|---|---|---|---|---|
| **1.** (c) | **2.** (c) | **3.** (a) | **4.** (c) | **5.** (a) | **6.** (a) |
| **7.** (b) | **8.** (b) | **9.** (a) | **10.** (c) | **11.** (d) | **12.** (a) |

# Experiment 10

## AIM

To determine the speed of a pulse propagated through a stretched string/slinky (helical spring).

## Materials Required

A 1 to 5m long metal slinky/slinky of copper, a stopwatch/stopclock and a meter scale (measuring tape).

## Theory/Principle

### Pulse

A pulse is a small disturbance in a medium that usually of small size and also lasts for a very short interval of time (see Fig. 1). The motion of a pulse can be observed on a stretched string or slinky.

Pulses are classified according to the direction in which they disturbs the medium. A longitudinal pulse can be illustrated as the pulse in which particles of the medium vibrate in the direction of motion of the pulse.

**Fig. 1**

If the disturbance (or pulse) moves the particle of the medium at the right angles to the direction of motion of the pulse, then the pulse is transverse.

### Pulse Velocity

The velocity of pulse wave is defined as the distance travelled by the pulse from free end to another fixed end in unit time interval. It is also called wave velocity.

i.e. $$\text{Wave velocity } (v) = \frac{\text{Distance travelled by pulse}}{\text{Time taken}} = \frac{s}{t}$$

SI unit of wave velocity is m/s. Wave velocity is also given by the relation

$$\text{Wave velocity } (v) = \text{Wave frequency } (\nu) \times \text{Wavelength } (\lambda)$$

### Slinky

A slinky is a long soft and flexible spring (Fig. 2). Generally, it is made up of copper.

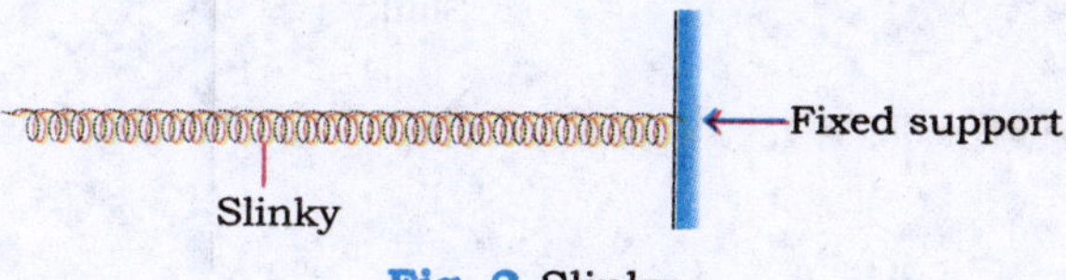


**Fig. 2** Slinky

A slinky can produce both transverse and longitudinal waves as shown in Fig. 3.

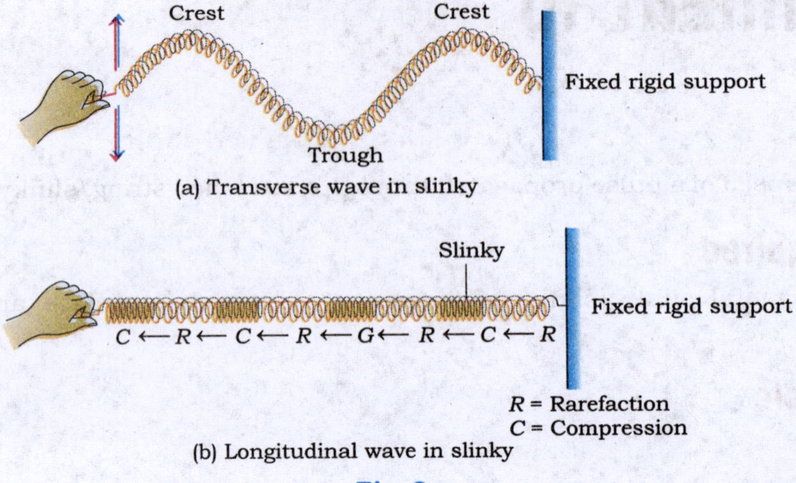


**Fig. 3**

Transverse wave can be produced along a slinky by providing sudden sharp uniform jerks at right angles to its length at free end of slinky. Longitudinal wave can be produced along a slinky by giving a forward and backward motion to its free end.

## Procedure

1. First of all note down the least count of stopwatch/stopclock.
2. Attach one end of the slinky to a rigid support (see Fig. 4).

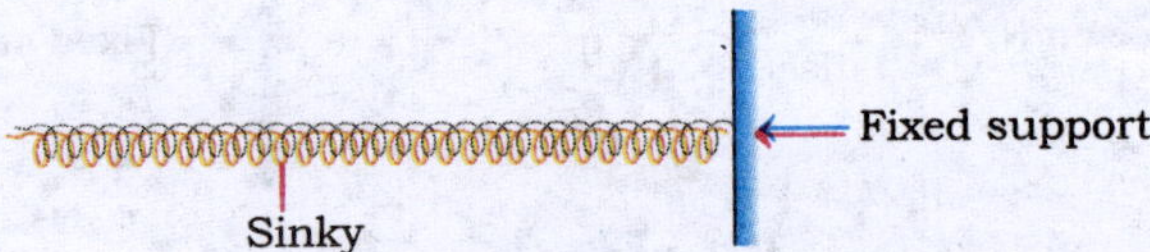


**Fig. 4** Slinky in normal condition

3. Now, measure the length of the slinky with the measuring tape by stretching it to some extent (approx. 1 cm).
4. Hold the slinky from its free end and create a disturbance up and down vertically (as in case of transverse wave, see Fig. 5).

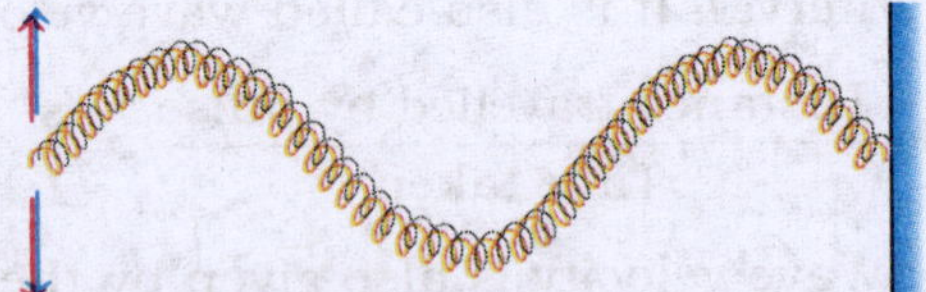

**Fig. 5** Transverse wave in slinky

5. Start the stopwatch at the instant you have created disturbance.
6. Note down the reading of stopwatch when the pulse reaches to the fixed support.
7. Now, again create a disturbance in a back and forth manner (as in case of longitudinal wave, see Fig. 6).

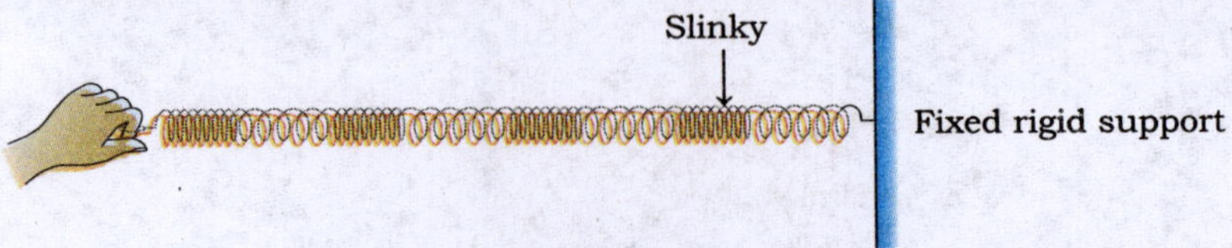


**Fig. 6** Longitudinal wave in slinky

8. Repeat steps 5 and 6 to note down the reading of stopwatch.
9. Do either of the steps 4 or 7, three to four times and note down the reading of stopwatch in observation table.

## Observations

Least count of stopwatch/stopclock = ......... s

Length of slinky ($s$) = ......... cm = ......... m

| S.N. | Total number of pulse produced ($N$) | Total time taken ($T$) | Time taken by one pulse, $t = T/N$ (s) | Velocity of pulse, $v = \frac{s}{t}$ (m/s) |
|---|---|---|---|---|
| 1. | 10 | | | $v_1$ = ... m/s |
| 2. | 15 | | | $v_2$ = ... m/s |
| 3. | 20 | | | $v_3$ = ... m/s |

## Calculations

Mean value of velocity of pulse, $v = \frac{v_1 + v_2 + v_3}{3}$ = ......... m/s

## Result

From the above observations and calculations, we conclude that the velocity of the pulse is ......... m/s.

### PRECAUTIONS

1. The slinky must be soft, long, massless and flexible.
2. Slinky must not be stretched to a large extent otherwise it will lose its spring capability.
3. Stopwatch must have a small least count.
4. One end of slinky must be fixed properly.
5. Recording of time must be taken carefully otherwise it may vary the velocity of pulse.
6. No part of the stretched slinky should touch the surface.
7. The slinky should not have any knot or kink at any point along its length.

## Sources of Error

1. Counting of pulse may not be calculated accurately.
2. Measurement of the slinky length may not be done accurately with measuring tape.
3. The student who starts and stops the stopwatch might be slow or fast each time.

## Suggested Experiments

1. Perform a similar experiment with the help of string and calculate the velocity of transverse pulse.
2. Suggest an activity to discuss the effects of air and other factors on the speed of pulse.

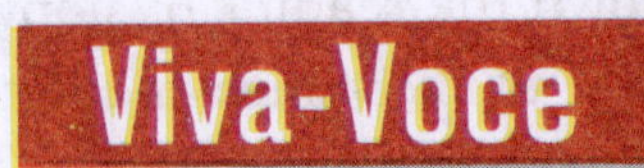

## Viva-Voce

**Q. 1 In which situation, one can sense a compression in a slinky?**

**Ans.** When turns in a slinky are close to one another than its original configuration, it signifies compression.

**Q. 2 Give the relationship between wavelength (λ), velocity (v) and frequency (ν).**

**Ans.** $v = \nu\lambda$

**Q. 3 What will be the velocity of the reflected pulse?**

**Ans.** The velocity of reflected pulse is same as that of incident pulse.

**Q. 4 Can you say the name of pulse produced when a stone is dropped on the surface of still water?**

**Ans.** The wave or pulse produced when a stone is dropped in still water will be transverse wave.

**Q. 5 Differentiate between transverse and longitudinal waves.**

**Ans.** Transverse wave consists of crests and troughs which are produced due to the movement of particles of the medium up and down at the right angle to the direction of propagation of wave.

Longitudinal wave consists of compressions and rarefactions which are produced due to the movement of particles of the medium to and fro about their mean position in the same direction in which the wave is propagated.

## Questions From NCERT Lab Manual

**Q. 1 What is the difference between pulse and wave?**

**Ans.** Pulse is produced by a single disturbance for very short duration, whereas waves are produced by continuous disturbances.

**Q. 2 State the nature of pulse generated in a stretched string. Is it transverse or longitudinal? Can a longitudinal pulse be generated in a string or a thread (an amateur's telephone)?**

**Ans.** The pulse generated in a stretched string is a transverse wave. Yes, a longitudinal pulse can also be produced in a string or a thread.

**Q. 3 Why do we prefer a longer string to perform the experiment?**

**Ans.** As we know that the, speed of pulse generated in slinky/string is very high and for small string, we will not be able to calculate the time taken by the pulse for a single journey, so we prefer longer string.

**Q. 4 In this experiment, you must have noticed that while expressing the result for the speed of a pulse in a string, it is not suggested to take the average value of speeds determined with different lengths of the string, why?**

**Ans.** The value of speed of pulse depends on the length of string as

$$v \propto \frac{1}{\sqrt{\mu}} \qquad \text{(where, } \mu = \text{mass/length)}$$

So, it is not suggested to take the average value of speeds determined with different lengths of the string.

**Q. 5 In this experiment, you are suggested to find the least count of the stopwatch or stopclock. At the same time, you are also using a meter scale or a measuring tape. But, you are not suggested to find the least count of this length measuring equipment. Why?**

**Ans.** The variation in time will have a large effect on the experimental calculations.

Also, the length we have considered in the experiment is too large for its variation to affect any change in the calculations.

**Q. 6 Why the release of gathered slinky coils be quick at the time of creation of a longitudinal pulse in the slinky?**

**Ans.** Pulse is a disturbance of very short duration, therefore it should be released quickly create on accurate pulse.

**Q. 7 How a longitudinal pulse travels in a slinky?**

**Ans.** A longitudinal pulse travels in the form of compressions and rarefactions.

**Q. 8 Why should you take a long slinky in this experiment?**

**Ans.** Long slinky is used to observe the change accurately, otherwise our reaction time will bring error in the observations.

**Q. 9 What will happen, if the middle portion of the stretched slinky touches a surface while a longitudinal pulse is travelling through it?**

**Ans.** The longitudinal wave will lose its energy at the point where the slinky touches the surface, and it may not travel further.

**Q.10 While creating a longitudinal pulse in the slinky instead of quickly and gently releasing the gathered coils, a student happens to move his hand, holding one end of slinky, sideways. What kind of pulse will be created in the slinky? Explain your answer.**

**Ans.** The slinky should be left quickly to produce a longitudinal pulse. If the student moves his hand, sideways a transverse pulse will also be created, having displacement perpendicular to the motion of the pulse. Thus, both the pulses will be visible.

**Q.11 In this experiment, you probably find different values of speed of a longitudinal pulse for different values of lengths of stretched slinky. Why?**

**Ans.** The speed of longitudinal pulse in a slinky is found to be inversely proportional to the square root of mass per unit length of slinky. Therefore, different values of lengths of stretched slinky have different values of speed.

**Q.12 Why do we measure time for larger number of pulse journeys in the stretched slinky, in this experiment?**

**Ans.** The speed of longitudinal pulse in a stretched slinky is quite high to measure the time taken by the pulse in a single journey. Therefore, larger number of pulse journeys are taken to reduce error.

## Practical Based MCQs

**Q. 1 When a pulse is formed on a slinky,**

(a) medium oscillates for a long time
(b) medium remains undisturbed
(c) medium oscillates for a short while and then returns to its original position
(d) Both (a) and (b)

**Q. 2 If the air in the room cools down, then the speed of sound**

(a) increases
(b) decreases
(c) remains the same
(d) fluctuates

**Q. 3** **We can sense a compression in a spring, if**

(a) turns are farther apart than normal (b) turns are closer than normal
(c) turns are neither close nor apart (d) None of the above

**Q. 4** **The stopwatch used by a student to measure velocity of a pulse in a slinky was of least count 0.1s. He stops the stopwatch, when a pulse has made 3 journeys from one end to the other of the slinky. He finds seconds hand to be at 47th division. What will be correct time?**

(a) 4.5 s (b) 4.2 s (c) 4.7 s (d) 4 s

**Q. 5** **Following figure shows a pulse generated in a string which moves through it and strikes a rigid pole.**

**What will be the direction of reflected pulse?**

(a) (b)

(c) (d) None of these

**Q. 6** **If stopwatch used makes *t* second, when pulse moves *n* times to and fro, what will be the time period of the motion of pulse?**

(a) $n \times t$ (b) $\frac{n}{t}$ (c) $\frac{t}{n}$ (d) None of these

**Q. 7** **A weight suspended from a spring is pulled downward and then released. What is produced in the spring?**

(a) Longitudinal wave (b) Periodic wave
(c) Transverse wave (d) None of these

**Q. 8** **The speed of propagation of a pulse in a slinky depends on**

(a) dimensions of slinky (b) material of slinky
(c) length of slinky (d) All of these

**Q. 9** **To find the velocity of the pulse produced in a string, what will be needed?**

(a) Measuring scale (b) Stopwatch
(c) Slinky (d) Both (a) and (b)

**Q.10** **While determining the velocity of propagation of pulse, which type of pulse is generated on the slinky in the experiment?**

(a) Longitudinal pulse (b) Transverse pulse
(c) Combination of (a) and (b) (d) None of these

**Q.11** **In the experiment for determining the velocity of a pulse propagating along the length of string, we prefer a long thick cotton string because**

(a) longer the string, less accurately we can measure the time
(b) longer the string, more accurately we can measure the time
(c) longer the string, less air resistance
(d) None of the above

## Answers

| | | | | | |
|---|---|---|---|---|---|
| **1.** (c) | **2.** (b) | **3.** (b) | **4.** (c) | **5.** (b) | **6.** (c) |
| **7.** (a) | **8.** (d) | **9.** (d) | **10.** (a) | **11.** (b) | |

# Experiment 11

## AIM

To verify the law of conservation of mass in a chemical reaction.

## Materials Required

A digital balance, two 200 mL beakers, $BaCl_2 \cdot 2H_2O$ solution, $Na_2SO_4 \cdot 10H_2O$ solution, 1 small test tube, conical flask, cork and distilled water.

## Theory/Principle

The **law of conservation of mass** states that "matter can neither be created nor destroyed".

From this principle, it follows that in a chemical reaction, total mass of reactants is equal to the total mass of products. In other words, the mass remains unchanged or conserved in a chemical reaction. This law is also known as **law of indestructibility of matter**.

In this experiment, we shall verify the law of conservation of mass using a precipitation reaction between sodium chloride [NaCl(*aq*)] and sodium sulphate [$Na_2SO_4(aq)$].

The reaction involved is

$$BaCl_2(aq) + Na_2SO_4(aq) \longrightarrow \underset{\text{white precipitate}}{BaSO_4(s)} \downarrow + 2NaCl(aq)$$

and more precisely

$$Ba^{2+}(aq) + SO_4^{2-}(aq) \longrightarrow BaSO_4(s)$$

## Procedure

1. Prepare a 5% solution of $BaCl_2$ and 5% solution of $Na_2SO_4$ in two separate beakers.
2. Take small amount (5 mL) of $Na_2SO_4$ in the conical flask.
3. Take a small test tube and put a little amount of $BaCl_2$ (2 mL) in it. Hang this small test tube carefully and make sure that the solution do not mix to each other (fig. 1).
4. Put a cork on the flask.
5. Weigh the flask with all the contents using the digital balance. Note it as $W_1$.
6. Now tie and swirl the flask such that the solution of $BaCl_2$ and $Na_2SO_4$ mix with each other.
7. Weigh the flask again and note it as $W_2$.

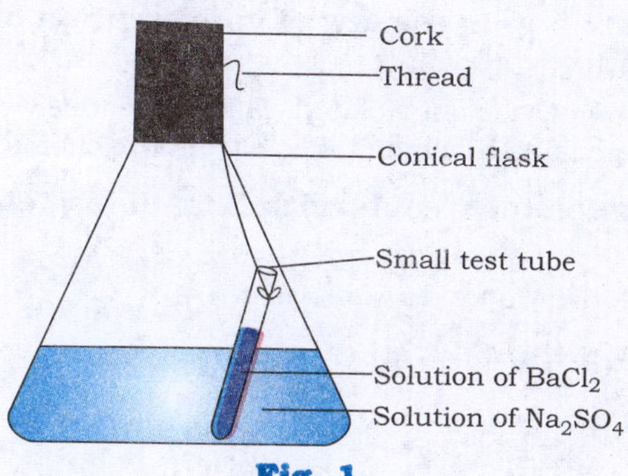


**Fig. 1**

## Observation

1. A reaction takes place between $BaCl_2$ and $Na_2SO_4$ and a white precipitate of $BaSO_4$ is formed.
2. $W_1$ and $W_2$ are equal.

## Result

On comparison of the masses of the reaction mixture, it is found that total mass of reactants (before reaction) is equal to the total mass of products (after reaction).

Above results verifies the law of the conservation of mass.

### PRECAUTIONS

1. The glass apparatus should be clean and dry.
2. The digital balance should be cleaned before use.
3. The readings of the digital balance should be noted carefully.
4. Do not taste salts of $BaCl_2$ and $Na_2SO_4$.
5. Two separate spatulas should be used for taking $BaCl_2$ and $Na_2SO_4$.
6. Mixing of $BaCl_2$ and $Na_2SO_4$ solutions be done slowly.

## Suggested Experiments

1. Verify the law of conservation of mass by using the precipitation reaction between silver nitrate ($AgNO_3$) and sodium chloride (NaCl).
2. Can a combination reaction also be used to prove the law of conservation of mass? Give an example and prove it.

# Viva-Voce

**Q. 1 What are the other precipitation reactions that can be conveniently studied in the laboratory to verify this law?**

**Ans.** Other precipitation reactions which can prove this law is a reaction between $AgNO_3(aq)$ and NaCl $(aq)$ as per the following equation

$$AgNO_3(aq) + NaCl\,(aq) \rightarrow \underset{\text{White ppt.}}{AgCl\,(s)\downarrow} + NaNO_3(aq)$$

**Q. 2 2 g of zinc metal is completely burned in air to form zinc oxide. It was found that mass of zinc oxide is 2.5 g. Is the law of conservation of mass violated? Explain your answer.**

**Ans.** The law of conservation of mass is not violated. This is because we have not taken into account the mass of gaseous oxygen (in air) which takes part in the chemical reaction as a reactant.

**Q. 3 4.0 g of hydrogen completely reacts with 32 g of oxygen. What will be the mass of water formed?**

**Ans.** Equation for the formation of water is as follows

$$H_2 + \frac{1}{2}O_2 \longrightarrow H_2O$$

$$4\text{ g} + 32\text{ g} \longrightarrow x$$

According to the law of conservation of mass,
Amount of water formed is,

$$x = (4 + 32)\text{g} = 36\text{g}$$

**Q. 4 On decomposition of 9.8g of $KClO_3$, The residue of KCl weighing 5.92 g is left behind along with oxygen. Find the mass of oxygen produced on decomposition.**

**Ans.** According to the law of conservation of mass,

Mass of $KClO_3$ = mass of oxygen + mass of KCl

Thus, mass of oxygen = $(9.8 - 5.92)\text{g} = 3.88\text{g}$

**Q. 5 To verify the law of conservation of mass in the case of a chemical reaction, sodium sulphate and barium chloride should be used in which form?**

**Ans.** Aqueous solution is used because precipitation reactions take place only when reactants are present in the aqueous state.

**Q. 6 Does the law of conservation of mass holds good for physical changes also?**

**Ans.** Yes, the law of conservation of mass holds good for physical changes too.

**Q. 7 Who was the first scientist to verify law of conservation of mass? Is there any relation between law of conservation of matter and law of conservation of mass?**

**Ans.** Antoine Lavoisier. Yes, law of conservation of mass is a special case of law of conservation of matter.

**Q. 8 If in an experiment, silver nitrate is used in the place of barium sulphate and sodium chloride is used in the place of sodium sulphate. Which reaction is used to verify, law of conservation of mass?**

**Ans.** When silver nitrate is reacted with sodium chloride, the precipitation reaction occurs and precipitate of AgCl formed.

**Q. 9 In nuclear reactions, why does law of conservation of mass not hold good?**

**Ans.** Because in nuclear reactions, mass is converted into energy according to the Einstein equation, $E = mc^2$.

**Q.10 In an experiment to verify the law of conservation of mass in a chemical reaction, we take one reactant in a small test tube and the other reactant in conical flask. Before chemical reaction to take place between these two reactants, why do we put a cork on the mouth of the flask and test tube?**

**Ans.** The cork is put, so that gaseous products do not escape and true reading can be recorded.

**Q.11 Give the name of any two laws of chemical combination.**

**Ans.** (i) Law of multiple proportion.
(ii) Law of conservation of mass.

**Q.12 What will be the colour of silver nitrate solution and sodium chloride solution?**

**Ans.** Both are colourless solutions.

## Practical Based MCQs

**Q. 1** **4 g of calcium completely reacts with 1.6 g of oxygen. What will be the mass of calcium oxide formed?**

(a) 3.6 g (b) 5.6 g (c) 2.4 g (d) 4.2 g

**Q. 2** **"The mass can neither be created nor destroyed in a chemical reaction". Which law is described by this statement?**

(a) Law of conservation of mass (b) Law of constant proportion
(c) Dalton' s atomic theory (d) Avogadro's law

**Q. 3** **1.25 g of copper carbonate was added to a beaker containing 20 g of HCl. After completion of a chemical reaction, the mass of the beaker and its contents were less than 21.25 g. Why does this happen?**

(a) Law of conservation of mass is not true in every case.
(b) Some atoms destroy during a reaction, hence reducing the mass.
(c) Some atoms (molecules) might have escaped during the reaction.
(d) Actual reason is not known.

**Q. 4** **3 g of magnesium ribbon burns completely in 2 g of oxygen to form magnesium oxide. What is the mass of magnesium oxide thus formed?**

(a) 5 g (b) 1 g (c) 6 g (d) 1.5 g

**Q. 5** **To verify the law of conservation of mass in the case of a chemical change, what form of sodium sulphate and barium chloride should be used?**

(a) Solid form (b) Liquid form
(c) Aqueous form (d) Any form gives same result

**Q. 6** **Law of conservation of mass is applicable to which types of changes?**

(a) All chemical changes (b) All physical changes
(c) All chemical and physical changes (d) Only some chemical changes

**Q. 7** **Which of the following reaction is preferred to verify law of conservation of mass?**

(a) Precipitation (b) Combination (c) Combustion (d) Substitution

**Q. 8** **4.0 g of hydrogen completely reacts with 32 g of oxygen. What will be the mass of water thus formed?**

(a) 18 g (b) 27 g (c) 36 g (d) 9 g

**Q. 9** **4.90 g of $KClO_3$, when heated produced 1.94 g of oxygen. What will be the mass of residue left?**

(a) 6.84 g (b) 4.90 g (c) 2.96 g (d) 1.94 g

**Q.10** **Two reactants kept in beaker as aqueous solution, weighs 200 g altogether. If beaker weighs 100 g, then find the total mass of product formed.**

(a) 200 g (b) 100 g (c) 300 g (d) 400 g

**Q.11** $$\underset{10\text{ g}}{AgNO_3(aq)} + \underset{5\text{ g}}{NaCl(aq)} \longrightarrow \underset{7\text{ g}}{AgCl(s)} + \underset{x}{NaNO_3(aq)}$$

**In the above reaction, what will be the amount of $NaNO_3$?**

(a) 8 g (b) 12 g (c) 15 g (d) 3 g

### Answers

| | | | | | |
|---|---|---|---|---|---|
| **1.** (b) | **2.** (a) | **3.** (c) | **4.** (a) | **5.** (c) | **6.** (c) |
| **7.** (a) | **8.** (c) | **9.** (c) | **10.** (b) | **11.** (a) | |

# LOGARITHMS

| N | 0 | 1 | 2 | 3 | 4 | 5 | 6 | 7 | 8 | 9 | Mean Differences 1 | 2 | 3 | 4 | 5 | 6 | 7 | 8 | 9 |
|---|---|---|---|---|---|---|---|---|---|---|---|---|---|---|---|---|---|---|---|
| 10 | 0000 | 0043 | 0086 | 0128 | 0170 | | | | | | 5 | 9 | 13 | 17 | 21 | 26 | 30 | 34 | 38 |
| | | | | | | 0212 | 0253 | 0294 | 0334 | 0374 | 4 | 8 | 12 | 16 | 20 | 24 | 28 | 32 | 36 |
| 11 | 0414 | 0453 | 0492 | 0531 | 0569 | | | | | | 4 | 8 | 12 | 16 | 20 | 23 | 27 | 31 | 35 |
| | | | | | | 0607 | 0645 | 0682 | 0719 | 0755 | 4 | 7 | 11 | 15 | 18 | 22 | 26 | 29 | 33 |
| 12 | 0792 | 0828 | 0864 | 0899 | 0934 | | | | | | 3 | 7 | 11 | 14 | 18 | 21 | 25 | 28 | 32 |
| | | | | | | 0969 | 1004 | 1038 | 1072 | 1106 | 3 | 7 | 10 | 14 | 17 | 20 | 24 | 27 | 31 |
| 13 | 1139 | 1173 | 1206 | 1239 | 1271 | | | | | | 3 | 6 | 10 | 13 | 16 | 19 | 23 | 26 | 29 |
| | | | | | | 1303 | 1335 | 1367 | 1399 | 1430 | 3 | 7 | 10 | 13 | 16 | 19 | 22 | 25 | 29 |
| 14 | 1461 | 1492 | 1523 | 1553 | 1584 | | | | | | 3 | 6 | 9 | 12 | 15 | 19 | 22 | 25 | 28 |
| | | | | | | 1614 | 1644 | 1673 | 1703 | 1732 | 3 | 6 | 9 | 12 | 14 | 17 | 20 | 23 | 26 |
| 15 | 1761 | 1790 | 1818 | 1847 | 1875 | | | | | | 3 | 6 | 9 | 11 | 14 | 17 | 20 | 23 | 26 |
| | | | | | | 1903 | 1931 | 1959 | 1987 | 2014 | 3 | 6 | 8 | 11 | 14 | 17 | 19 | 22 | 25 |
| 16 | 2041 | 2068 | 2095 | 2122 | 2148 | | | | | | 3 | 6 | 8 | 11 | 14 | 16 | 19 | 22 | 24 |
| | | | | | | 2175 | 2201 | 2227 | 2253 | 2279 | 3 | 5 | 8 | 10 | 13 | 16 | 18 | 21 | 23 |
| 17 | 2304 | 2330 | 2355 | 2380 | 2405 | | | | | | 3 | 5 | 8 | 10 | 13 | 15 | 18 | 20 | 23 |
| | | | | | | 2430 | 2455 | 2480 | 2504 | 2529 | 3 | 5 | 8 | 10 | 12 | 15 | 17 | 20 | 22 |
| 18 | 2553 | 2577 | 2601 | 2625 | 2648 | | | | | | 2 | 5 | 7 | 9 | 12 | 14 | 17 | 19 | 21 |
| | | | | | | 2672 | 2695 | 2718 | 2742 | 2765 | 2 | 4 | 7 | 9 | 11 | 14 | 16 | 18 | 21 |
| 19 | 2788 | 2810 | 2833 | 2856 | 2878 | | | | | | 2 | 4 | 7 | 9 | 11 | 13 | 16 | 18 | 20 |
| | | | | | | 2900 | 2923 | 2945 | 2967 | 2989 | 2 | 4 | 6 | 8 | 11 | 13 | 15 | 17 | 19 |
| **20** | 3010 | 3032 | 3054 | 3075 | 3096 | 3118 | 3139 | 3160 | 3181 | 3201 | 2 | 4 | 6 | 8 | 11 | 13 | 15 | 17 | 19 |
| 21 | 3222 | 3243 | 3263 | 3284 | 3304 | 3324 | 3345 | 3365 | 3385 | 3404 | 2 | 4 | 6 | 8 | 10 | 12 | 14 | 16 | 18 |
| 22 | 3424 | 3444 | 3464 | 3483 | 3502 | 3522 | 3541 | 3560 | 3579 | 3598 | 2 | 4 | 6 | 8 | 10 | 12 | 14 | 15 | 17 |
| 23 | 3617 | 3636 | 3655 | 3674 | 3692 | 3711 | 3729 | 3747 | 3766 | 3784 | 2 | 4 | 6 | 7 | 9 | 11 | 13 | 15 | 17 |
| 24 | 3802 | 3820 | 3838 | 3856 | 3874 | 3892 | 3909 | 3927 | 3945 | 3962 | 2 | 4 | 5 | 7 | 9 | 11 | 12 | 14 | 16 |
| 25 | 3979 | 3997 | 4014 | 4031 | 4048 | 4065 | 4082 | 4099 | 4116 | 4133 | 2 | 3 | 5 | 7 | 9 | 10 | 12 | 14 | 15 |
| 26 | 4150 | 4166 | 4183 | 4200 | 4216 | 4232 | 4249 | 4265 | 4281 | 4298 | 2 | 3 | 5 | 7 | 8 | 10 | 11 | 13 | 15 |
| 27 | 4314 | 4330 | 4346 | 4362 | 4378 | 4393 | 4409 | 4425 | 4440 | 4456 | 2 | 3 | 5 | 6 | 8 | 9 | 11 | 13 | 14 |
| 28 | 4472 | 4487 | 4502 | 4518 | 4533 | 4548 | 4564 | 4579 | 4594 | 4609 | 2 | 3 | 5 | 6 | 8 | 9 | 11 | 12 | 14 |
| 29 | 4624 | 4639 | 4654 | 4669 | 4683 | 4698 | 4713 | 4728 | 4742 | 4757 | 1 | 3 | 4 | 6 | 7 | 9 | 10 | 12 | 13 |
| **30** | 4771 | 4786 | 4800 | 4814 | 4829 | 4843 | 4857 | 4871 | 4886 | 4900 | 1 | 3 | 4 | 6 | 7 | 9 | 10 | 11 | 13 |
| 31 | 4914 | 4928 | 4942 | 4955 | 4969 | 4983 | 4997 | 5011 | 5024 | 5038 | 1 | 3 | 4 | 6 | 7 | 8 | 10 | 11 | 12 |
| 32 | 5051 | 5065 | 5079 | 5092 | 5105 | 5119 | 5132 | 5145 | 5159 | 5172 | 1 | 3 | 4 | 5 | 7 | 8 | 9 | 11 | 12 |
| 33 | 5185 | 5198 | 5211 | 5224 | 5237 | 5250 | 5263 | 5276 | 5289 | 5302 | 1 | 3 | 4 | 5 | 6 | 8 | 9 | 10 | 12 |
| 34 | 5315 | 5328 | 5340 | 5353 | 5366 | 5378 | 5391 | 5403 | 5416 | 5428 | 1 | 3 | 4 | 5 | 6 | 8 | 9 | 10 | 11 |
| **35** | 5441 | 5453 | 5465 | 5478 | 5490 | 5502 | 5514 | 5527 | 5539 | 5551 | 1 | 2 | 4 | 5 | 6 | 7 | 9 | 10 | 11 |
| 36 | 5563 | 5575 | 5587 | 5599 | 5611 | 5623 | 5635 | 5647 | 5658 | 5670 | 1 | 2 | 4 | 5 | 6 | 7 | 8 | 10 | 11 |
| 37 | 5682 | 5694 | 5705 | 5717 | 5729 | 5740 | 5752 | 5763 | 5775 | 5786 | 1 | 2 | 3 | 5 | 6 | 7 | 8 | 9 | 10 |
| 38 | 5798 | 5809 | 5821 | 5832 | 5843 | 5855 | 5866 | 5877 | 5888 | 5899 | 1 | 2 | 3 | 5 | 6 | 7 | 8 | 9 | 10 |
| 39 | 5911 | 5922 | 5933 | 5944 | 5955 | 5966 | 5977 | 5988 | 5999 | 6010 | 1 | 2 | 3 | 4 | 5 | 7 | 8 | 9 | 10 |
| **40** | 6021 | 6031 | 6042 | 6053 | 6064 | 6075 | 6085 | 6096 | 6107 | 6117 | 1 | 2 | 3 | 4 | 5 | 6 | 8 | 9 | 10 |
| 41 | 6128 | 6138 | 6149 | 6160 | 6170 | 6180 | 6191 | 6201 | 6212 | 6222 | 1 | 2 | 3 | 4 | 5 | 6 | 7 | 8 | 9 |
| 42 | 6232 | 6243 | 6253 | 6263 | 6274 | 6284 | 6294 | 6304 | 6314 | 6325 | 1 | 2 | 3 | 4 | 5 | 6 | 7 | 8 | 9 |
| 43 | 6335 | 6345 | 6355 | 6365 | 6375 | 6385 | 6395 | 6405 | 6415 | 6425 | 1 | 2 | 3 | 4 | 5 | 6 | 7 | 8 | 9 |
| 44 | 6435 | 6444 | 6454 | 6464 | 6474 | 6484 | 6493 | 6503 | 6513 | 6522 | 1 | 2 | 3 | 4 | 5 | 6 | 7 | 8 | 9 |
| **45** | 6532 | 6542 | 6551 | 6561 | 6571 | 6580 | 6590 | 6599 | 6609 | 6618 | 1 | 2 | 3 | 4 | 5 | 6 | 7 | 8 | 9 |
| 46 | 6628 | 6637 | 6646 | 6656 | 6665 | 6675 | 6684 | 6693 | 6702 | 6712 | 1 | 2 | 3 | 4 | 5 | 6 | 7 | 7 | 8 |
| 47 | 6721 | 6730 | 6739 | 6749 | 6758 | 6767 | 6776 | 6785 | 6794 | 6803 | 1 | 2 | 3 | 4 | 5 | 5 | 6 | 7 | 8 |
| 48 | 6812 | 6821 | 6830 | 6839 | 6848 | 6857 | 6866 | 6875 | 6884 | 6893 | 1 | 2 | 3 | 4 | 4 | 5 | 6 | 7 | 8 |
| 49 | 6902 | 6911 | 6920 | 6928 | 6937 | 6946 | 6955 | 6964 | 6972 | 6981 | 1 | 2 | 3 | 4 | 4 | 5 | 6 | 7 | 8 |
| **50** | 6990 | 6998 | 7007 | 7016 | 7024 | 7033 | 7042 | 7050 | 7059 | 7067 | 1 | 2 | 3 | 3 | 4 | 5 | 6 | 7 | 8 |

## LOGARITHMS (CONTD.)

| | 0 | 1 | 2 | 3 | 4 | 5 | 6 | 7 | 8 | 9 | Mean Differences | | | | | | | | |
|---|---|---|---|---|---|---|---|---|---|---|---|---|---|---|---|---|---|---|---|
| | | | | | | | | | | | 1 | 2 | 3 | 4 | 5 | 6 | 7 | 8 | 9 |
| 51 | 7076 | 7084 | 7093 | 7101 | 7110 | 7118 | 7126 | 7135 | 7143 | 7152 | 1 | 2 | 3 | 3 | 4 | 5 | 6 | 7 | 8 |
| 52 | 7160 | 7168 | 7177 | 7185 | 7193 | 7202 | 7210 | 7218 | 7226 | 7235 | 1 | 2 | 2 | 3 | 4 | 5 | 6 | 7 | 7 |
| 53 | 7243 | 7251 | 7259 | 7267 | 7275 | 7284 | 7292 | 7300 | 7308 | 7316 | 1 | 2 | 2 | 3 | 4 | 5 | 6 | 6 | 7 |
| 54 | 7324 | 7332 | 7340 | 7348 | 7356 | 7364 | 7372 | 7380 | 7388 | 7396 | 1 | 2 | 2 | 3 | 4 | 5 | 6 | 6 | 7 |
| **55** | 7404 | 7412 | 7419 | 7427 | 7435 | 7443 | 7451 | 7459 | 7466 | 7474 | 1 | 2 | 2 | 3 | 4 | 5 | 5 | 6 | 7 |
| 56 | 7482 | 7490 | 7497 | 7505 | 7513 | 7520 | 7528 | 7536 | 7543 | 7551 | 1 | 2 | 2 | 3 | 4 | 5 | 5 | 6 | 7 |
| 57 | 7559 | 7566 | 7574 | 7582 | 7589 | 7597 | 7604 | 7612 | 7619 | 7627 | 1 | 2 | 2 | 3 | 4 | 5 | 5 | 6 | 7 |
| 58 | 7634 | 7642 | 7649 | 7657 | 7664 | 7672 | 7679 | 7686 | 7694 | 7701 | 1 | 2 | 2 | 3 | 4 | 4 | 5 | 6 | 7 |
| 59 | 7709 | 7716 | 7723 | 7731 | 7738 | 7745 | 7752 | 7760 | 7767 | 7774 | 1 | 1 | 2 | 3 | 4 | 4 | 5 | 6 | 7 |
| **60** | 7782 | 7789 | 7796 | 7803 | 7810 | 7818 | 7825 | 7832 | 7839 | 7846 | 1 | 1 | 2 | 3 | 4 | 4 | 5 | 6 | 6 |
| 61 | 7853 | 7860 | 7868 | 7875 | 7882 | 7889 | 7896 | 7903 | 7910 | 7917 | 1 | 1 | 2 | 3 | 4 | 4 | 5 | 6 | 6 |
| 62 | 7924 | 7931 | 7938 | 7945 | 7952 | 7959 | 7966 | 7973 | 7980 | 7987 | 1 | 1 | 2 | 3 | 3 | 4 | 5 | 6 | 6 |
| 63 | 7993 | 8000 | 8007 | 8014 | 8021 | 8028 | 8035 | 8041 | 8048 | 8055 | 1 | 1 | 2 | 3 | 3 | 4 | 5 | 5 | 6 |
| 64 | 8062 | 8069 | 8075 | 8082 | 8089 | 8096 | 8102 | 8109 | 8116 | 8122 | 1 | 1 | 2 | 3 | 3 | 4 | 5 | 5 | 6 |
| **65** | 8129 | 8136 | 8142 | 8149 | 8156 | 8162 | 8169 | 8176 | 8182 | 8189 | 1 | 1 | 2 | 3 | 3 | 4 | 5 | 5 | 6 |
| 66 | 8195 | 8202 | 8209 | 8215 | 8222 | 8228 | 8235 | 8241 | 8248 | 8254 | 1 | 1 | 2 | 3 | 3 | 4 | 5 | 5 | 6 |
| 67 | 8261 | 8267 | 8274 | 8280 | 8287 | 8293 | 8299 | 8306 | 8312 | 8319 | 1 | 1 | 2 | 3 | 3 | 4 | 5 | 5 | 6 |
| 68 | 8325 | 8331 | 8338 | 8344 | 8351 | 8357 | 8363 | 8370 | 8376 | 8382 | 1 | 1 | 2 | 3 | 3 | 4 | 4 | 5 | 6 |
| 69 | 8388 | 8395 | 8401 | 8407 | 8414 | 8420 | 8426 | 8432 | 8439 | 8445 | 1 | 1 | 2 | 2 | 3 | 4 | 4 | 5 | 6 |
| **70** | 8451 | 8457 | 8463 | 8470 | 8476 | 8482 | 8488 | 8494 | 8500 | 8506 | 1 | 1 | 2 | 2 | 3 | 4 | 4 | 5 | 6 |
| 71 | 8513 | 8519 | 8525 | 8531 | 8537 | 8543 | 8549 | 8555 | 8561 | 8567 | 1 | 1 | 2 | 2 | 3 | 4 | 4 | 5 | 5 |
| 72 | 8573 | 8579 | 8585 | 8591 | 8597 | 8603 | 8609 | 8615 | 8621 | 8627 | 1 | 1 | 2 | 2 | 3 | 4 | 4 | 5 | 5 |
| 73 | 8633 | 8639 | 8645 | 8651 | 8657 | 8663 | 8669 | 8675 | 8681 | 8686 | 1 | 1 | 2 | 2 | 3 | 4 | 4 | 5 | 5 |
| 74 | 8692 | 8698 | 8704 | 8710 | 8716 | 8722 | 8727 | 8733 | 8739 | 8745 | 1 | 1 | 2 | 2 | 3 | 4 | 4 | 5 | 5 |
| **75** | 8751 | 8756 | 8762 | 8768 | 8774 | 8779 | 8785 | 8791 | 8797 | 8802 | 1 | 1 | 2 | 2 | 3 | 3 | 4 | 5 | 5 |
| 76 | 8808 | 8814 | 8820 | 8825 | 8831 | 8837 | 8842 | 8848 | 8854 | 8859 | 1 | 1 | 2 | 2 | 3 | 3 | 4 | 5 | 5 |
| 77 | 8865 | 8871 | 8876 | 8882 | 8887 | 8893 | 8899 | 8904 | 8910 | 8915 | 1 | 1 | 2 | 2 | 3 | 3 | 4 | 4 | 5 |
| 78 | 8921 | 8927 | 8932 | 8938 | 8943 | 8949 | 8954 | 8960 | 8965 | 8971 | 1 | 1 | 2 | 2 | 3 | 3 | 4 | 4 | 5 |
| 79 | 8976 | 8982 | 8987 | 8993 | 8998 | 9004 | 9009 | 9015 | 9020 | 9025 | 1 | 1 | 2 | 2 | 3 | 3 | 4 | 4 | 5 |
| **80** | 9031 | 9036 | 9042 | 9047 | 9053 | 9058 | 9063 | 9069 | 9074 | 9079 | 1 | 1 | 2 | 2 | 3 | 3 | 4 | 4 | 5 |
| 81 | 9085 | 9090 | 9096 | 9101 | 9106 | 9112 | 9117 | 9122 | 9128 | 9133 | 1 | 1 | 2 | 2 | 3 | 3 | 4 | 4 | 5 |
| 82 | 9138 | 9143 | 9149 | 9154 | 9159 | 9165 | 9170 | 9175 | 9180 | 9186 | 1 | 1 | 2 | 2 | 3 | 3 | 4 | 4 | 5 |
| 83 | 9191 | 9196 | 9201 | 9206 | 9212 | 9217 | 9222 | 9227 | 9232 | 9238 | 1 | 1 | 2 | 2 | 3 | 3 | 4 | 4 | 5 |
| 84 | 9243 | 9248 | 9253 | 9258 | 9263 | 9269 | 9274 | 9279 | 9284 | 9289 | 1 | 1 | 2 | 2 | 3 | 3 | 4 | 4 | 5 |
| **85** | 9294 | 9299 | 9304 | 9309 | 9315 | 9320 | 9325 | 9330 | 9335 | 9340 | 1 | 1 | 2 | 2 | 3 | 3 | 4 | 4 | 5 |
| 86 | 9345 | 9350 | 9355 | 9360 | 9365 | 9370 | 9375 | 9380 | 9385 | 9390 | 1 | 1 | 2 | 2 | 3 | 3 | 4 | 4 | 5 |
| 87 | 9395 | 9400 | 9405 | 9410 | 9415 | 9420 | 9425 | 9430 | 9435 | 9440 | 0 | 1 | 1 | 2 | 2 | 3 | 3 | 4 | 4 |
| 88 | 9445 | 9450 | 9455 | 9460 | 9465 | 9469 | 9474 | 9479 | 9484 | 9489 | 0 | 1 | 1 | 2 | 2 | 3 | 3 | 4 | 4 |
| 89 | 9494 | 9499 | 9504 | 9509 | 9513 | 9518 | 9523 | 9528 | 9533 | 9538 | 0 | 1 | 1 | 2 | 2 | 3 | 3 | 4 | 4 |
| **90** | 9542 | 9547 | 9552 | 9557 | 9562 | 9566 | 9571 | 9576 | 9581 | 9586 | 0 | 1 | 1 | 2 | 2 | 3 | 3 | 4 | 4 |
| 91 | 9590 | 9595 | 9600 | 9605 | 9609 | 9614 | 9619 | 9624 | 9628 | 9633 | 0 | 1 | 1 | 2 | 2 | 3 | 3 | 4 | 4 |
| 92 | 9638 | 9643 | 9647 | 9652 | 9657 | 9661 | 9666 | 9671 | 9675 | 9680 | 0 | 1 | 1 | 2 | 2 | 3 | 3 | 4 | 4 |
| 93 | 9685 | 9689 | 9694 | 9699 | 9703 | 9708 | 9713 | 9717 | 9722 | 9727 | 0 | 1 | 1 | 2 | 2 | 3 | 3 | 4 | 4 |
| 94 | 9731 | 9736 | 9741 | 9745 | 9750 | 9754 | 9759 | 9763 | 9788 | 9773 | 0 | 1 | 1 | 2 | 2 | 3 | 3 | 4 | 4 |
| **95** | 9777 | 9782 | 9786 | 9791 | 9795 | 9800 | 9805 | 9809 | 9814 | 9818 | 0 | 1 | 1 | 2 | 2 | 3 | 3 | 4 | 4 |
| 96 | 9823 | 9827 | 9832 | 9836 | 9841 | 9845 | 9850 | 9854 | 9859 | 9863 | 0 | 1 | 1 | 2 | 2 | 3 | 3 | 4 | 4 |
| 97 | 9868 | 9872 | 9877 | 9881 | 9886 | 9890 | 9894 | 9899 | 9903 | 9908 | 0 | 1 | 1 | 2 | 2 | 3 | 3 | 4 | 4 |
| 98 | 9912 | 9917 | 9921 | 9926 | 9930 | 9934 | 9939 | 9943 | 9948 | 9952 | 0 | 1 | 1 | 2 | 2 | 3 | 3 | 4 | 4 |
| 99 | 9956 | 9961 | 9965 | 9969 | 9974 | 9978 | 9983 | 9987 | 9991 | 9996 | 0 | 1 | 1 | 2 | 2 | 3 | 3 | 3 | 4 |

# ANTILOGARITHMS

| | 0 | 1 | 2 | 3 | 4 | 5 | 6 | 7 | 8 | 9 | Mean Differences | | | | | | | | |
|---|---|---|---|---|---|---|---|---|---|---|---|---|---|---|---|---|---|---|---|
| | | | | | | | | | | | 1 | 2 | 3 | 4 | 5 | 6 | 7 | 8 | 9 |
| .00 | 1000 | 1002 | 1005 | 1007 | 1009 | 1012 | 1014 | 1016 | 1019 | 1021 | 0 | 0 | 1 | 1 | 1 | 1 | 2 | 2 | 2 |
| .01 | 1023 | 1026 | 1028 | 1030 | 1033 | 1035 | 1038 | 1040 | 1042 | 1045 | 0 | 0 | 1 | 1 | 1 | 1 | 2 | 2 | 2 |
| .02 | 1047 | 1050 | 1052 | 1054 | 1057 | 1059 | 1062 | 1064 | 1067 | 1069 | 0 | 0 | 1 | 1 | 1 | 1 | 2 | 2 | 2 |
| .03 | 1072 | 1074 | 1076 | 1079 | 1081 | 1084 | 1086 | 1089 | 1091 | 1094 | 0 | 0 | 1 | 1 | 1 | 1 | 2 | 2 | 2 |
| .04 | 1096 | 1099 | 1102 | 1104 | 1107 | 1109 | 1112 | 1114 | 1117 | 1119 | 0 | 1 | 1 | 1 | 1 | 2 | 2 | 2 | 2 |
| **.05** | 1122 | 1125 | 1127 | 1130 | 1132 | 1135 | 1138 | 1140 | 1143 | 1146 | 0 | 1 | 1 | 1 | 1 | 2 | 2 | 2 | 2 |
| .06 | 1148 | 1151 | 1153 | 1156 | 1159 | 1161 | 1164 | 1167 | 1169 | 1172 | 0 | 1 | 1 | 1 | 1 | 2 | 2 | 2 | 2 |
| .07 | 1175 | 1178 | 1180 | 1183 | 1186 | 1189 | 1191 | 1194 | 1197 | 1199 | 0 | 1 | 1 | 1 | 1 | 2 | 2 | 2 | 2 |
| .08 | 1202 | 1205 | 1208 | 1211 | 1213 | 1216 | 1219 | 1222 | 1225 | 1227 | 0 | 1 | 1 | 1 | 1 | 2 | 2 | 2 | 3 |
| .09 | 1230 | 1233 | 1236 | 1239 | 1242 | 1245 | 1247 | 1250 | 1253 | 1256 | 0 | 1 | 1 | 1 | 1 | 2 | 2 | 2 | 3 |
| **.10** | 1259 | 1262 | 1265 | 1268 | 1271 | 1274 | 1276 | 1279 | 1282 | 1285 | 0 | 1 | 1 | 1 | 1 | 2 | 2 | 2 | 3 |
| .11 | 1288 | 1291 | 1294 | 1297 | 1300 | 1303 | 1306 | 1309 | 1312 | 1315 | 0 | 1 | 1 | 1 | 2 | 2 | 2 | 2 | 3 |
| .12 | 1318 | 1321 | 1324 | 1327 | 1330 | 1334 | 1337 | 1340 | 1343 | 1346 | 0 | 1 | 1 | 1 | 2 | 2 | 2 | 2 | 3 |
| .13 | 1349 | 1352 | 1355 | 1358 | 1361 | 1365 | 1368 | 1371 | 1374 | 1377 | 0 | 1 | 1 | 1 | 2 | 2 | 2 | 3 | 3 |
| .14 | 1380 | 1384 | 1387 | 1390 | 1393 | 1396 | 1400 | 1403 | 1406 | 1409 | 0 | 1 | 1 | 1 | 2 | 2 | 2 | 3 | 3 |
| **.15** | 1413 | 1416 | 1419 | 1422 | 1426 | 1429 | 1432 | 1435 | 1439 | 1442 | 0 | 1 | 1 | 1 | 2 | 2 | 2 | 3 | 3 |
| .16 | 1445 | 1449 | 1452 | 1455 | 1459 | 1462 | 1466 | 1469 | 1472 | 1476 | 0 | 1 | 1 | 1 | 2 | 2 | 2 | 3 | 3 |
| .17 | 1479 | 1483 | 1486 | 1489 | 1493 | 1496 | 1500 | 1503 | 1507 | 1510 | 0 | 1 | 1 | 1 | 2 | 2 | 2 | 3 | 3 |
| .18 | 1514 | 1517 | 1521 | 1524 | 1528 | 1531 | 1535 | 1538 | 1542 | 1545 | 0 | 1 | 1 | 1 | 2 | 2 | 2 | 3 | 3 |
| .19 | 1549 | 1552 | 1556 | 1560 | 1563 | 1567 | 1570 | 1574 | 1578 | 1581 | 0 | 1 | 1 | 1 | 2 | 2 | 3 | 3 | 3 |
| **.20** | 1585 | 1589 | 1592 | 1596 | 1600 | 1603 | 1607 | 1611 | 1614 | 1618 | 0 | 1 | 1 | 1 | 2 | 2 | 3 | 3 | 3 |
| .21 | 1622 | 1626 | 1629 | 1633 | 1637 | 1641 | 1644 | 1648 | 1652 | 1656 | 0 | 1 | 1 | 2 | 2 | 2 | 3 | 3 | 3 |
| .22 | 1660 | 1663 | 1667 | 1671 | 1675 | 1679 | 1683 | 1687 | 1690 | 1694 | 0 | 1 | 1 | 2 | 2 | 2 | 3 | 3 | 3 |
| .23 | 1698 | 1702 | 1706 | 1710 | 1714 | 1718 | 1722 | 1726 | 1730 | 1734 | 0 | 1 | 1 | 2 | 2 | 2 | 3 | 3 | 4 |
| .24 | 1738 | 1742 | 1746 | 1750 | 1754 | 1758 | 1762 | 1766 | 1770 | 1774 | 0 | 1 | 1 | 2 | 2 | 2 | 3 | 3 | 4 |
| **.25** | 1778 | 1782 | 1786 | 1791 | 1795 | 1799 | 1803 | 1807 | 1811 | 1816 | 0 | 1 | 1 | 2 | 2 | 2 | 3 | 3 | 4 |
| .26 | 1820 | 1824 | 1828 | 1832 | 1837 | 1841 | 1845 | 1849 | 1854 | 1858 | 0 | 1 | 1 | 2 | 2 | 3 | 3 | 3 | 4 |
| .27 | 1862 | 1866 | 1871 | 1875 | 1879 | 1884 | 1888 | 1892 | 1897 | 1901 | 0 | 1 | 1 | 2 | 2 | 3 | 3 | 3 | 4 |
| .28 | 1905 | 1910 | 1914 | 1919 | 1923 | 1928 | 1932 | 1936 | 1941 | 1945 | 0 | 1 | 1 | 2 | 2 | 3 | 3 | 4 | 4 |
| .29 | 1950 | 1954 | 1959 | 1963 | 1968 | 1972 | 1977 | 1982 | 1986 | 1991 | 0 | 1 | 1 | 2 | 2 | 3 | 3 | 4 | 4 |
| **.30** | 1995 | 2000 | 2004 | 2009 | 2014 | 2018 | 2023 | 2028 | 2032 | 2037 | 0 | 1 | 1 | 2 | 2 | 3 | 3 | 4 | 4 |
| .31 | 2042 | 2046 | 2051 | 2056 | 2061 | 2065 | 2070 | 2075 | 2080 | 2084 | 0 | 1 | 1 | 2 | 2 | 3 | 3 | 4 | 4 |
| .32 | 2089 | 2094 | 2099 | 2104 | 2109 | 2113 | 2118 | 2123 | 2128 | 2133 | 0 | 1 | 1 | 2 | 2 | 3 | 3 | 4 | 4 |
| .33 | 2138 | 2143 | 2148 | 2153 | 2158 | 2163 | 2168 | 2173 | 2178 | 2183 | 0 | 1 | 1 | 2 | 2 | 3 | 3 | 4 | 4 |
| .34 | 2188 | 2193 | 2198 | 2203 | 2208 | 2213 | 2218 | 2223 | 2228 | 2234 | 1 | 1 | 2 | 2 | 3 | 3 | 4 | 4 | 5 |
| **.35** | 2239 | 2244 | 2249 | 2254 | 2259 | 2265 | 2270 | 2275 | 2280 | 2286 | 1 | 1 | 2 | 2 | 3 | 3 | 4 | 4 | 5 |
| .36 | 2291 | 2296 | 2301 | 2307 | 2312 | 2317 | 2323 | 2328 | 2333 | 2339 | 1 | 1 | 2 | 2 | 3 | 3 | 4 | 4 | 5 |
| .37 | 2344 | 2350 | 2355 | 2360 | 2366 | 2371 | 2377 | 2382 | 2388 | 2393 | 1 | 1 | 2 | 2 | 3 | 3 | 4 | 4 | 5 |
| .38 | 2399 | 2404 | 2410 | 2415 | 2421 | 2427 | 2432 | 2438 | 2443 | 2449 | 1 | 1 | 2 | 2 | 3 | 3 | 4 | 4 | 5 |
| .39 | 2455 | 2460 | 2466 | 2472 | 2477 | 2483 | 2489 | 2495 | 2500 | 2506 | 1 | 1 | 2 | 2 | 3 | 3 | 4 | 5 | 5 |
| **.40** | 2512 | 2518 | 2523 | 2529 | 2535 | 2541 | 2547 | 2553 | 2559 | 2564 | 1 | 1 | 2 | 2 | 3 | 4 | 4 | 5 | 5 |
| .41 | 2570 | 2576 | 2582 | 2588 | 2594 | 2600 | 2696 | 2612 | 2618 | 2624 | 1 | 1 | 2 | 2 | 3 | 4 | 4 | 5 | 5 |
| .42 | 2630 | 2636 | 2642 | 2649 | 2655 | 2661 | 2667 | 2673 | 2679 | 2685 | 1 | 1 | 2 | 2 | 3 | 4 | 4 | 5 | 6 |
| .43 | 2692 | 2698 | 2704 | 2710 | 2716 | 2723 | 2729 | 2735 | 2742 | 2748 | 1 | 1 | 2 | 3 | 3 | 4 | 4 | 5 | 6 |
| .44 | 2754 | 2761 | 2767 | 2773 | 2780 | 2786 | 2793 | 2799 | 2805 | 2812 | 1 | 1 | 2 | 3 | 3 | 4 | 4 | 5 | 6 |
| **.45** | 2818 | 2825 | 2831 | 2838 | 2844 | 2851 | 2858 | 2864 | 2871 | 2877 | 1 | 1 | 2 | 3 | 3 | 4 | 5 | 5 | 6 |
| .46 | 2884 | 2891 | 2897 | 2904 | 2911 | 2917 | 2924 | 2931 | 2938 | 2944 | 1 | 1 | 2 | 3 | 3 | 4 | 5 | 5 | 6 |
| .47 | 2951 | 2958 | 2965 | 2972 | 2979 | 2985 | 2992 | 2999 | 3006 | 3013 | 1 | 1 | 2 | 3 | 3 | 4 | 5 | 5 | 6 |
| .48 | 3020 | 3027 | 3034 | 3041 | 3048 | 3055 | 3062 | 3069 | 3076 | 3083 | 1 | 1 | 2 | 3 | 4 | 4 | 5 | 6 | 6 |
| .49 | 3090 | 3097 | 3105 | 3112 | 3119 | 3126 | 3133 | 3141 | 3148 | 3155 | 1 | 1 | 2 | 3 | 4 | 4 | 5 | 6 | 6 |

## ANTILOGARITHMS (CONTD.)

| | 0 | 1 | 2 | 3 | 4 | 5 | 6 | 7 | 8 | 9 | Mean Differences | | | | | | | | |
|---|---|---|---|---|---|---|---|---|---|---|---|---|---|---|---|---|---|---|---|
| | | | | | | | | | | | 1 | 2 | 3 | 4 | 5 | 6 | 7 | 8 | 9 |
| **.50** | 3162 | 3170 | 3177 | 3184 | 3192 | 3199 | 3206 | 3214 | 3221 | 3228 | 1 | 1 | 2 | 3 | 4 | 4 | 5 | 6 | 7 |
| .51 | 3236 | 3243 | 3251 | 3258 | 3266 | 3273 | 3281 | 3289 | 3296 | 3304 | 1 | 2 | 2 | 3 | 4 | 5 | 5 | 6 | 7 |
| .52 | 3311 | 3319 | 3327 | 3334 | 3342 | 3350 | 3357 | 3365 | 3373 | 3381 | 1 | 2 | 2 | 3 | 4 | 5 | 5 | 6 | 7 |
| .53 | 3388 | 3396 | 3404 | 3412 | 3420 | 3428 | 3436 | 3443 | 3451 | 3459 | 1 | 2 | 2 | 3 | 4 | 5 | 6 | 6 | 7 |
| .54 | 3467 | 3475 | 3483 | 3491 | 3499 | 3508 | 3516 | 3524 | 3532 | 3540 | 1 | 2 | 2 | 3 | 4 | 5 | 6 | 6 | 7 |
| **.55** | 3548 | 3556 | 3565 | 3573 | 3581 | 3589 | 3597 | 3606 | 3614 | 3622 | 1 | 2 | 2 | 3 | 4 | 5 | 6 | 7 | 7 |
| .56 | 3631 | 3639 | 3648 | 3656 | 3664 | 3673 | 3681 | 3690 | 3698 | 3707 | 1 | 2 | 3 | 3 | 4 | 5 | 6 | 7 | 8 |
| .57 | 3715 | 3724 | 3733 | 3741 | 3750 | 3758 | 3767 | 3776 | 3784 | 3793 | 1 | 2 | 3 | 3 | 4 | 5 | 6 | 7 | 8 |
| .58 | 3802 | 3811 | 3819 | 3828 | 3837 | 3846 | 3855 | 3864 | 3873 | 3882 | 1 | 2 | 3 | 4 | 4 | 5 | 6 | 7 | 8 |
| .59 | 3890 | 3899 | 3908 | 3917 | 3926 | 3936 | 3945 | 3954 | 3963 | 3972 | 1 | 2 | 3 | 4 | 5 | 5 | 6 | 7 | 8 |
| **.60** | 3981 | 3990 | 3999 | 4009 | 4018 | 4027 | 4036 | 4046 | 4055 | 4064 | 1 | 2 | 3 | 4 | 5 | 6 | 6 | 7 | 8 |
| .61 | 4074 | 4083 | 4093 | 4102 | 4111 | 4121 | 4130 | 4140 | 4150 | 4159 | 1 | 2 | 3 | 4 | 5 | 6 | 7 | 8 | 9 |
| .62 | 4169 | 4178 | 4188 | 4198 | 4207 | 4217 | 4227 | 4236 | 4256 | 4256 | 1 | 2 | 3 | 4 | 5 | 6 | 7 | 8 | 9 |
| .63 | 4266 | 4276 | 4285 | 4295 | 4305 | 4315 | 4325 | 4335 | 4345 | 4355 | 1 | 2 | 3 | 4 | 5 | 6 | 7 | 8 | 9 |
| .64 | 4365 | 4375 | 4385 | 4395 | 4406 | 4416 | 4426 | 4436 | 4446 | 4457 | 1 | 2 | 3 | 4 | 5 | 6 | 7 | 8 | 9 |
| **.65** | 4467 | 4477 | 4487 | 4498 | 4508 | 4519 | 4529 | 4539 | 4550 | 4560 | 1 | 2 | 3 | 4 | 5 | 6 | 7 | 8 | 9 |
| .66 | 4571 | 4581 | 4592 | 4603 | 4613 | 4624 | 4634 | 4645 | 4656 | 4667 | 1 | 2 | 3 | 4 | 5 | 6 | 7 | 9 | 10 |
| .67 | 4677 | 4688 | 4699 | 4710 | 4721 | 4732 | 4742 | 4753 | 4764 | 4775 | 1 | 2 | 3 | 4 | 5 | 7 | 8 | 9 | 10 |
| .68 | 4786 | 4797 | 4808 | 4819 | 4831 | 4842 | 4853 | 4864 | 4875 | 4887 | 1 | 2 | 3 | 4 | 6 | 7 | 8 | 9 | 10 |
| .69 | 4898 | 4909 | 4920 | 4932 | 4943 | 4955 | 4966 | 4977 | 4989 | 5000 | 1 | 2 | 3 | 5 | 6 | 7 | 8 | 9 | 10 |
| **.70** | 5012 | 5023 | 5035 | 5047 | 5058 | 5070 | 5082 | 5093 | 5105 | 5117 | 1 | 2 | 4 | 5 | 6 | 7 | 8 | 9 | 11 |
| .71 | 5129 | 5140 | 5152 | 5164 | 5176 | 5188 | 5200 | 5212 | 5224 | 5236 | 1 | 2 | 4 | 5 | 6 | 7 | 8 | 10 | 11 |
| .72 | 5248 | 5260 | 5272 | 5284 | 5297 | 5309 | 5321 | 5333 | 5346 | 5358 | 1 | 2 | 4 | 5 | 6 | 7 | 9 | 10 | 11 |
| .73 | 5370 | 5383 | 5395 | 5408 | 5420 | 5433 | 5445 | 5458 | 5470 | 5483 | 1 | 3 | 4 | 5 | 6 | 8 | 9 | 10 | 11 |
| .74 | 5495 | 5508 | 5521 | 5534 | 5546 | 5559 | 5572 | 5585 | 5598 | 5610 | 1 | 3 | 4 | 5 | 6 | 8 | 9 | 10 | 12 |
| **.75** | 5623 | 5636 | 5649 | 5662 | 5675 | 5689 | 5702 | 5715 | 5728 | 5741 | 1 | 3 | 4 | 5 | 7 | 8 | 9 | 10 | 12 |
| .76 | 5754 | 5768 | 5781 | 5794 | 5808 | 5821 | 5834 | 5848 | 5861 | 5875 | 1 | 3 | 4 | 5 | 7 | 8 | 9 | 11 | 12 |
| .77 | 5888 | 5902 | 5916 | 5929 | 5943 | 5957 | 5970 | 5984 | 5998 | 6012 | 1 | 3 | 4 | 5 | 7 | 8 | 10 | 11 | 12 |
| .78 | 6026 | 6039 | 6053 | 6067 | 6081 | 6095 | 6109 | 6124 | 6138 | 6152 | 1 | 3 | 4 | 6 | 7 | 8 | 10 | 11 | 13 |
| .79 | 6166 | 6180 | 6194 | 6209 | 6223 | 7237 | 6252 | 6266 | 6281 | 6295 | 1 | 3 | 4 | 6 | 7 | 9 | 10 | 11 | 13 |
| **.80** | 6310 | 6324 | 6339 | 6353 | 6368 | 6383 | 6497 | 6412 | 6427 | 6442 | 1 | 3 | 4 | 6 | 7 | 9 | 10 | 12 | 13 |
| .81 | 6457 | 6471 | 6486 | 6501 | 6516 | 6531 | 6546 | 6561 | 6577 | 6592 | 2 | 3 | 5 | 6 | 8 | 9 | 11 | 12 | 14 |
| .82 | 6607 | 6622 | 6637 | 6653 | 6668 | 6683 | 6699 | 6714 | 6730 | 6745 | 2 | 3 | 5 | 6 | 8 | 9 | 11 | 12 | 14 |
| .83 | 6761 | 6776 | 6792 | 6808 | 6823 | 6839 | 6855 | 6871 | 6887 | 6902 | 2 | 3 | 5 | 6 | 8 | 9 | 11 | 13 | 14 |
| .84 | 6918 | 6934 | 6950 | 6966 | 6982 | 6998 | 7015 | 7031 | 7047 | 7063 | 2 | 3 | 5 | 6 | 8 | 10 | 11 | 13 | 15 |
| **.85** | 7079 | 7096 | 7112 | 7129 | 7145 | 7161 | 7178 | 7194 | 7211 | 7228 | 2 | 3 | 5 | 7 | 8 | 10 | 12 | 13 | 15 |
| .86 | 7244 | 7261 | 7278 | 7295 | 7311 | 7328 | 7345 | 7362 | 7379 | 7396 | 2 | 3 | 5 | 7 | 8 | 10 | 12 | 13 | 15 |
| .87 | 7413 | 7430 | 7447 | 7464 | 7482 | 7499 | 7516 | 7534 | 7551 | 7568 | 2 | 3 | 5 | 7 | 9 | 10 | 12 | 14 | 16 |
| .88 | 7586 | 7603 | 7621 | 7638 | 7656 | 7674 | 7691 | 7709 | 7727 | 7745 | 2 | 4 | 5 | 7 | 9 | 11 | 12 | 14 | 16 |
| .89 | 7762 | 7780 | 7798 | 7816 | 7834 | 7852 | 7870 | 7889 | 7907 | 7925 | 2 | 4 | 5 | 7 | 9 | 11 | 13 | 14 | 16 |
| **.90** | 7943 | 7962 | 7980 | 7998 | 8017 | 8035 | 8054 | 8072 | 8091 | 8110 | 2 | 4 | 6 | 7 | 9 | 11 | 13 | 15 | 17 |
| .91 | 8128 | 8147 | 8166 | 8185 | 8204 | 8222 | 8241 | 8260 | 8279 | 8299 | 2 | 4 | 6 | 8 | 9 | 11 | 13 | 15 | 17 |
| .92 | 8318 | 8337 | 8356 | 8375 | 8395 | 8414 | 8433 | 8453 | 8472 | 8492 | 2 | 4 | 6 | 8 | 10 | 12 | 14 | 15 | 17 |
| .93 | 8511 | 8531 | 8551 | 8570 | 8590 | 8610 | 8630 | 8650 | 8670 | 8690 | 2 | 4 | 6 | 8 | 10 | 12 | 14 | 16 | 18 |
| .94 | 8710 | 8730 | 8750 | 8770 | 8790 | 8810 | 8831 | 8851 | 8872 | 8892 | 2 | 4 | 6 | 8 | 10 | 12 | 15 | 17 | 19 |
| **.95** | 8913 | 8933 | 8954 | 8974 | 8995 | 9016 | 9036 | 9057 | 9078 | 9099 | 2 | 4 | 6 | 8 | 10 | 12 | 15 | 17 | 19 |
| .96 | 9120 | 9141 | 9162 | 9183 | 9204 | 9226 | 9247 | 9268 | 9290 | 9311 | 2 | 4 | 6 | 8 | 11 | 13 | 15 | 17 | 19 |
| .97 | 9333 | 9354 | 9376 | 9397 | 9419 | 9441 | 9462 | 9484 | 9506 | 9528 | 2 | 4 | 7 | 9 | 11 | 13 | 15 | 17 | 20 |
| .98 | 9550 | 9572 | 9594 | 9616 | 9638 | 9661 | 9683 | 9705 | 9727 | 9750 | 2 | 4 | 7 | 9 | 11 | 13 | 16 | 18 | 20 |
| .99 | 9772 | 9795 | 9817 | 9840 | 9863 | 9886 | 9908 | 9931 | 9954 | 9977 | 2 | 5 | 7 | 9 | 11 | 14 | 16 | 18 | 20 |

Experiment/Activity No.________ Date ________ Page No. ________

Teacher Signature ________________

Experiment/Activity No.________ Date ________ Page No. ________

Teacher Signature ________

Experiment/Activity No.________ Date ________ Page No. ________

Teacher Signature ________________

Experiment/Activity No.________ Date ________ Page No. ________

Teacher Signature________________

Experiment/Activity No.________ Date ________ Page No. ________

Teacher Signature ________________

Experiment/Activity No.________ Date ________ Page No. ________

Teacher Signature ________________

Experiment/Activity No.________ Date ________ Page No. ________

Teacher Signature________________

Experiment/Activity No.________ Date ________ Page No. ________

Teacher Signature________________

Experiment/Activity No.________ Date ________ Page No. ________

Teacher Signature ________________

Experiment/Activity No.________ Date ________ Page No. ________

Teacher Signature ________________

Experiment/Activity No.________ Date ________ Page No. ________

Teacher Signature ________

Experiment/Activity No.________ Date ________ Page No. ________

Teacher Signature ________________

Experiment/Activity No.________ Date ________ Page No. ________

Teacher Signature ________

Experiment/Activity No.________ Date ________ Page No. ________

Teacher Signature________________

Experiment/Activity No.________ Date ________ Page No. ________

Teacher Signature ________________

Experiment/Activity No.________ Date ________ Page No. ________

Teacher Signature ________________

Experiment/Activity No.________ Date ________ Page No. ________

Teacher Signature ________

Experiment/Activity No.________ Date ________ Page No. ________

Teacher Signature ________________

Experiment/Activity No.________ Date ________ Page No. ________

Teacher Signature ________________

Experiment/Activity No.________ Date ________ Page No. ________

Teacher Signature________________

Experiment/Activity No.________ Date ________ Page No. ________

Teacher Signature ________________

Experiment/Activity No.________ Date ________ Page No. ________

Teacher Signature ________________

Experiment/Activity No.________ Date ________ Page No. ________

Teacher Signature ________________

Experiment/Activity No.________ Date ________ Page No. ________

Teacher Signature ________________

Experiment/Activity No.________ Date ________ Page No. ________

Teacher Signature ____________

Experiment/Activity No.________ Date ________ Page No. ________

Teacher Signature ________________

Experiment/Activity No.________ Date ________ Page No. ________

Teacher Signature ____________

Experiment/Activity No.________ Date ________ Page No. ________

Teacher Signature ________

Experiment/Activity No.________ Date ________ Page No. ________

Teacher Signature ________________

Experiment/Activity No.________ Date ________ Page No. ________

Teacher Signature ________

Experiment/Activity No.________ Date ________ Page No. ________

Teacher Signature ________

Experiment/Activity No.________ Date ________ Page No. ________

Teacher Signature ________________

Experiment/Activity No.________ Date ________ Page No. ________

Teacher Signature________________

Experiment/Activity No.________ Date ________ Page No. ________

Teacher Signature ________________

Experiment/Activity No.________ Date ________ Page No. ________

Teacher Signature ________________

Experiment/Activity No.________ Date ________ Page No. ________

Teacher Signature ________________

Experiment/Activity No.________ Date ________ Page No. ________

Teacher Signature ________________

Experiment/Activity No.________ Date ________ Page No. ________

Teacher Signature ________________

Experiment/Activity No.________ Date ________ Page No. ________

Teacher Signature ________________

Experiment/Activity No.________ Date ________ Page No. ________

Teacher Signature ________

Experiment/Activity No.________ Date ________ Page No. ________

Teacher Signature________

Experiment/Activity No.________ Date ________ Page No. ________

Teacher Signature ________________

Experiment/Activity No.________ Date ________ Page No. ________

Teacher Signature ________________

Experiment/Activity No.________ Date ________ Page No. ________

Teacher Signature ________

Experiment/Activity No.________ Date ________ Page No. ________

Teacher Signature ________

Experiment/Activity No.________ Date ________ Page No. ________

Teacher Signature ________

Experiment/Activity No.________ Date ________ Page No. ________

Teacher Signature ________________

Experiment/Activity No.________ Date ________ Page No. ________

Teacher Signature ________________

Experiment/Activity No.________ Date ________ Page No. ________

Teacher Signature ________

Experiment/Activity No.________ Date ________ Page No. ________

Teacher Signature ________________

Experiment/Activity No.________ Date ________ Page No. ________

Teacher Signature ________________

Experiment/Activity No.________ Date ________ Page No. ________

Teacher Signature________________

Experiment/Activity No.________ Date ________ Page No. ________

Teacher Signature ________________

Experiment/Activity No.________ Date ________ Page No. ________

Teacher Signature ________________

Experiment/Activity No.________ Date ________ Page No. ________

Teacher Signature ________________

Experiment/Activity No.________ Date ________ Page No. ________

Teacher Signature ________________

Experiment/Activity No.________ Date ________ Page No. ________

Teacher Signature ________

Experiment/Activity No.________ Date ________ Page No. ________

Teacher Signature ________________

Experiment/Activity No.________ Date ________ Page No. ________

Teacher Signature ________________

Experiment/Activity No.________ Date ________ Page No. ________

Teacher Signature ________________

Experiment/Activity No.________ Date ________ Page No. ________

Teacher Signature ________________

Experiment/Activity No.________ Date ________ Page No. ________

Teacher Signature ________________

Experiment/Activity No.________ Date ________ Page No. ________

Teacher Signature ________________

Experiment/Activity No.________ Date ________ Page No. ________

Teacher Signature ________________